VALUES

•Activities •Ideas •Strategies

Grades 2-3

Published with the permission of R.I.C. Publications Pty. Ltd.

Copyright © 2007 by Didax, Inc., Rowley, MA 01969. All rights reserved.

First published by R.I.C. Publications Pty. Ltd., Perth, Western Australia. Revised by Didax Educational Resources.

Printed in the United States of America.

Order Number: 2-5284
ISBN-13: 978-1-58324-266-7

A B C D E F 11 10 09 08 07

395 Main Street
Rowley, MA 01969
www.didax.com

FOREWORD

Values education in schools is crucial for developing future citizens of good character. The *Values* series, featuring the *Six Kinds of Best* concept, is expressly designed to assist the teaching of values education in elementary and middle schools. The varied activities in this book extend across all major learning areas and will have relevance for a wide range of student learning styles and intelligences.

Titles in this series are:
- *Values — Grades K to 1*
- *Values — Grades 2 to 3*
- *Values — Grades 4 to 5*
- *Values — Grades 6 to 8*

CONTENTS

TEACHER NOTES

What Are Values?

Values are ideals that guide our behavior and decisions and help us distinguish between what is right or wrong. They outline what is important to us in terms of our conduct, our interaction with others and how we might live our lives in a meaningful way. Values give us a guiding framework by which to lead our lives. People who engage in antisocial behavior often lack a values framework.

Why Teach Values?

Developing good values gives us a structure to guide our conscience and helps us make good choices. If we have strong values and are put in challenging situations, we are more likely to make good decisions according to those values. Developing strong values also helps address our spiritual needs and self-esteem by giving us a personal sense of identity and direction. In addition, it helps develop a sense of responsibility for the consequences of our own behavior and the awareness of how our actions might affect ourselves, others and the environment.

Teaching values in schools is a proactive approach toward managing student behavior. It gives students effective strategies to help them lead happy and successful lives.

Values can be incorporated into a whole-school approach and can include:

- *Encouraging staff to model good values.*
- *Including values in the school vision and mission statements.*
- *Creating a school motto, slogan or ethos based on specific values.*
- *Displaying values posters.*
- *Including values in school rules and policies.*
- *Including values in structured classroom guidelines such as class rules.*
- *Introducing ongoing daily or weekly values programs.*
- *Integrating the teaching of values into all curriculum learning areas.*
- *Collating and using resources for specific values education lessons.*
- *Inviting guest speakers to the school.*
- *Teaching values incidentally during class or recess times.*

Values education encourages students to become "nice human beings."

Values Within School Curriculums

Generally speaking, there are nine agreed values to be incorporated into school curriculums.

These are:
Care and compassion
Doing your best
"Being fair"
Freedom
Honesty and trustworthiness
Integrity
Respect
Responsibility
Understanding, tolerance and inclusion

The **"Six Kinds of Best"** concept incorporates all these values.

The "Six Kinds of Best" Concept

The "Six Kinds of Best" is a model that outlines six core values for becoming a person of good character and for leading a happy and successful life. It frames the core values in a way that students, teachers and parents can remember and apply in everyday situations. It provides "anchor points" upon which we can reflect when faced with decision-making situations and will help us make good choices. It may be considered a "recipe for life."

The **"Six Kinds of Best"** are:

Be KIND to Yourself .... (Respect yourself)
Be KIND to Others .... (Respect others)
Be KIND to the Environment .... (Value the environment)
Be the Learning KIND .... (Seek knowledge)
Be the Achieving KIND .... (Achieve your potential)
Be the Community KIND .... (Contribute positively to society)

TEACHER NOTES

The "Six Kinds of Best" concept uses a play on the word "kind" to make it memorable and repeatable. It also reinforces the word "kind." It provides a mechanism to continually reinforce good values and teach them in context.

This book is divided into six sections to indicate the six core values. Each section has a number of pointers which illustrate and support the six values.

The "Six Kinds of Best" concept provides a framework and a language for teaching and reinforcing values at school and in the home. It aims to make students familiar with the six core values and to internalize them by using the "Six Kinds of Best" **affirmation**. (Refer to page 9, the cover pages of each section and page 135.)

Teachers and parents are encouraged to highlight incorrect behaviors and reinforce correct behaviors by using the language of the "Six Kinds of Best."

These six fingers represent the "Six Kinds of Best." Get your students to make the sign. Tell them if they apply these principles throughout their life, they will be "A-OK."

Make the "Six Kinds of Best" your personal quest

For example:

- When a student makes a negative comment about himself/herself, the teacher may say, *"Sasha, you're not being kind to yourself, are you?"*

- When one student bullies another, the teacher may say, *"John! You're not being kind to others, are you?"*

- When a student drops some trash, the teacher may comment about the child not being *"kind to the environment."*

- When the class does well in a test, the teacher may comment that they are really *"the learning kind."*

- When a student does an assignment well, the teacher may say that the student is *"the achieving kind."*

- When a group of students helps to clean up, the teacher may state that they are *"the community kind."*

Using This Book

The activities in this book may be:

   — Incorporated into a continuing weekly program.

   — Used incidentally as required in the classroom.

   — Incorporated into an existing personal development or values program.

   — Used in conjunction with special values events such as a values "supercharger" day or values "week" where a guest speaker works with the students.

TEACHER NOTES

The book is divided into six sections. The six sections are:

- *Be Kind to Yourself*
- *Be Kind to Others*
- *Be Kind to the Environment*
- *Be the Learning Kind*
- *Be the Achieving Kind*
- *Be the Community Kind*

Title Page

The first page of each section is a title page designed to introduce the section.

- A *pictorial representation of the affirmation(s)* is/are also supplied.

Overview

A two-page overview of additional activities has been provided for each of the six sections. The activities cover a variety of learning areas and learning styles. Teachers may use the activities to further develop each section with the class or as extension work for more able students.

Teacher Notes Pages

The student pages are supported by two pages of *Teacher Notes*, which are comprised of:

- An introduction to the section,
- A compilation of discussion points for each student page and
- Answers (where required).

Each double teacher page also includes one or more examples of a *graphic organizer,* which teachers may find beneficial for recording summaries of students' discussion or for students to record their thoughts. Graphic organizers provide a visual representation of information. They employ four intelligences at the same time—verbal/linguistic, logical/mathematical, visual/spatial and naturalist. (Different organizers use aspects of the naturalist intelligence, including categorizing, classifying, identifying, etc.)

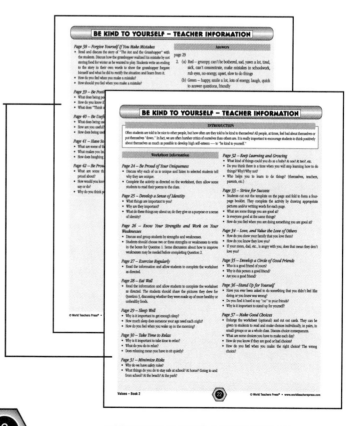

TEACHER NOTES

Student Pages

Each section is divided into a number of **key pointers**. The key points are utilized as individual **student pages**. The activities on the student pages are intended to be mostly open-ended, "fun" tasks focusing on the **eight multiple intelligences**.

Each student page includes:
— The title of the relevant section.
— Title of the student page.

Be Kind to Yourself – Be Proud of Your Uniqueness

The One and Only!

1. Read the poem.

> I am special. I am unique.
> You won't find another, no matter how hard you seek.
> I'm not like you. You're not like me.
> But it keeps life interesting, as you will see!

2. Use the dictionary to write the meaning of the word *unique*.

3. Write words and phrases which tell why you are unique; e.g. freckled, friendly, a good joke teller, etc.

4. Use some of the words above to write an acrostic poem about yourself telling why you are unique.

U
N
I
Q
U
E

Values – Book 2   24   © World Teachers Press® • www.worldteacherspress.com

The final four pages in the book include:

— A pictorial representation of the "I Love Life" affirmation.

— A chatterbox template, to help reinforce concepts from this book.

— A bibliography of references and suggested readings to further teacher knowledge and appropriate Web sites.

Additional Information

Discussion and student reflection about their own personal experiences form an important part of values education. For this reason, discussion points form a major portion of the teacher information section of teacher notes for each section.

> By applying the "Six Kinds of Best" principles, students and adults will lead a happy, successful and fulfilling life and they will feel like saying "I love life!"

David Koutsoukis is the creator of the "*Six Kinds of Best*" concept. He is an educator with over 20 years' experience who has a passion for encouraging people to develop good values and become persons of good character. He is also the author of the *Behavior Management Toolkit*, the R.I.C. *Behavior Management* and *Values* poster sets, and the *Daily Dose of Fun* series of books.

David is now a full-time presenter and consultant who works with educators, helping them build positive school cultures. He conducts professional development programs for teachers throughout Australia, New Zealand and Southeast Asia on how to effectively deliver the *Six Kinds of Best* program. David also does a motivational program for students entitled *Make the Six Kinds of Best Your Personal Quest*.

Internet Web sites

In some cases, Web sites or specific URLs may be recommended. While these are checked and rechecked at the time of publication, the publisher has no control over any subsequent changes which may be made to Web pages. It is *strongly* recommended that the class teacher checks *all* URLs before allowing students to access them.

THE SIX KINDS OF BEST

Values Framework

SIX CORE VALUES

1. Be KIND to Yourself *Respect Yourself*	2. Be KIND to Others *Respect Others*	3. Be KIND to the Environment *Value the Environment*	4. Be the Learning KIND *Seek Knowledge*	5. Be the Achieving KIND *Achieve Your Potential*	6. Be the Community KIND *Contribute Positively to Society*
KEY POINTERS					
1. Be proud of your uniqueness.	1. Value relationships.	1. Clean up after yourself.	1. Be positive about learning.	1. Giving it a try!	1. Behave responsibly.
2. Develop a sense of identity *(know what is important to you)*.	2. Respect the rights of others.	2. Keep the land, air and waterways clean.	2. Seek knowledge about yourself, others and the world around you.	2. Try lots of different things.	2. Respect authority.
3. Know your strengths and work on your weaknesses.	3. Be polite and use good manners.	3. Recycle and don't waste.	3. Recognize the value of knowledge.	3. Discover what you're good at and enjoy doing.	3. Follow rules.
4. Exercise regularly.	4. Praise people who do things well.	4. Save water.	4. Have an enquiring mind *(be curious)*.	4. Do things to the best of your ability.	4. Be honest and seek the truth.
5. Eat well.	5. Develop good people skills.	5. Conserve energy.	5. Determine how you learn best *(learning styles)*.	5. Pursue quality and personal excellence.	5. Show integrity *(develop a sense of what's morally right and act that way)*.
6. Sleep well.	6. Work at building and maintaining relationships.	6. Care for natural habitats, wildlife and endangered species.	6. Have an open mind.	6. Use your talents.	6. Be useful.
7. Take time to relax.	7. Be tolerant and understanding of difference.	7. Use environmentally-friendly products.	7. Be a critical thinker.	7. Develop a sense of purpose.	7. Get involved in the community.
8. Minimize risks.	8. Respect other points of view.	8. Consider environmentally friendly energy sources.	8. Have a global perspective.	8. Manage your time effectively.	8. Strive for justice and a fair chance for all.
9. Keep learning and growing.	9. Don't bully or put others down.	9. Consider using resources that can be replaced *(sustainable development)*.	9. Seek learning opportunities everywhere.	9. Manage your money wisely.	9. Share and care for those in need.
10. Strive for success *(and get some ego food)*.	10. Seek a fair chance for all.	10. Value our cultural heritage.	10. Learn from your mistakes.	10. Set worthwhile goals and make plans to achieve them.	10. Support reconciliation.
11. Love, and value the love of others.	11. Manage and resolve conflict.		11. Keep learning.	11. Show persistence and self-discipline to achieve your goals.	11. Contribute to research.
12. Develop a circle of good friends.	12. Cooperate and be a team player.			12. Look at different ways of doing things *(creativity and innovation)*.	12. Support freedom.
13. Stand up for yourself *(be confident but humble)*.	13. Support and include others.			13. Develop good communication skills.	13. Strive for peace.
14. Make good choices.	14. Value family life.			14. Seek good role models.	
15. Forgive yourself if you make mistakes.	15. Treat others the way they need to be treated.				
16. Be positive.					
17. Be useful *(and you will feel good about yourself)*.					
18. Have some fun.					
19. Be proud of the things you say and do.					

THE "SIX KINDS OF BEST" AFFIRMATION

The "Six Kinds of Best" affirmation is a series of actions which reinforces the six core values in a memorable and fun way. Reciting the affirmation engages visual, auditory and kinesthetic learners.

I am one of a kind.
(Right index finger in the air in front of body.)

I am kind to myself.
(Clenched fist over heart.)

I am kind to others.
(From clenched fist over heart, swing right arm clockwise and point outwards.)

And I am kind to the environment.
(American Sign Language for the letter "E.")

I am the learning kind.
(Have left hand flat, palm upwards, waist height—like a book. Take right hand and sweep the left hand with the back of your hand and swing your hand up to touch the top of your head—putting the information from the book into your head.)

I am the achieving kind.
(Point upwards—aim for the stars.)

And I am the community kind.
(Form an "A" shape in front of your body with your fingers—like a house.)

And I
(Point to yourself and touch your chest.)

Love
(Hug yourself.)

Life!
(Hands and arms outstretched above your head.)

MAKE "THE SIX KINDS OF BEST" YOUR PERSONAL QUEST!

BE KIND TO OTHERS

This award is presented to

for

Teacher

Date

MAKE "THE SIX KINDS OF BEST" YOUR PERSONAL QUEST!

BE KIND TO OTHERS

This award is presented to

for

Teacher

Date

CERTIFICATES

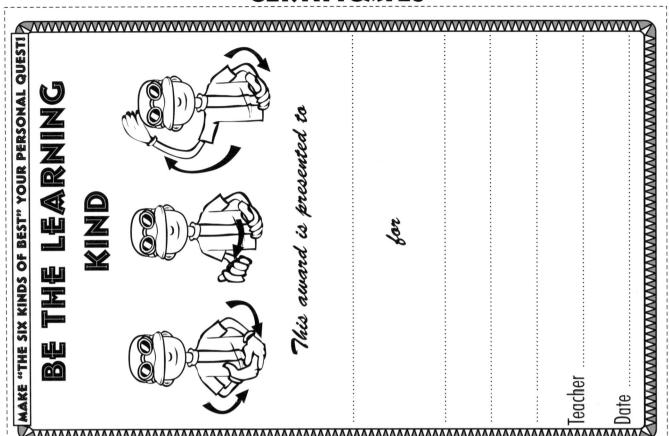

MAKE "THE SIX KINDS OF BEST" YOUR PERSONAL QUEST!

BE THE LEARNING KIND

This award is presented to

for

Teacher ....

Date ....

MAKE "THE SIX KINDS OF BEST" YOUR PERSONAL QUEST!

BE THE LEARNING KIND

This award is presented to

for

Teacher ....

Date ....

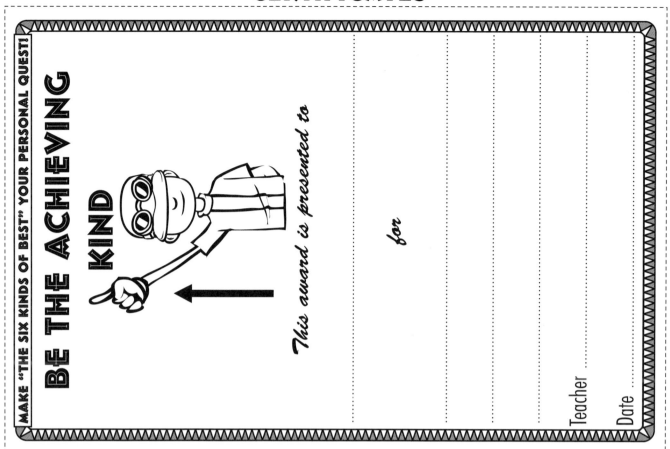

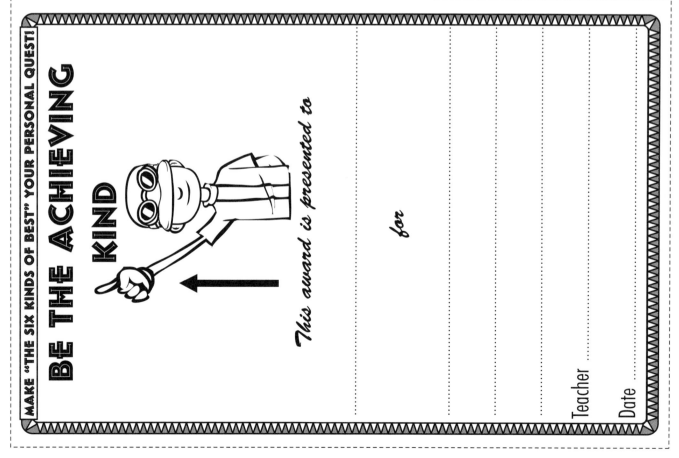

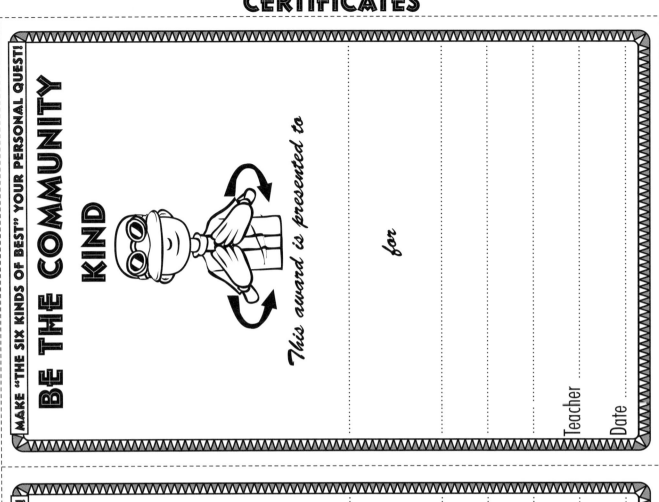

"SIX KINDS OF BEST" CHECKLISTS

Teacher – Student Self-Reflection Checklist

Name _____

Go through the list, check the appropriate boxes and see how you rate. You will notice a profile that will indicate which of your values are strongly developed, and which areas you need to improve.

❶ Be Kind to Yourself	Strongly Agree	Agree	Disagree	Strongly Disagree
1. I am proud of my uniqueness.				
2. I have a strong sense of identity.				
3. I know my strengths and work on my weaknesses.				
4. I exercise regularly.				
5. I eat well.				
6. I sleep well.				
7. I take time to relax.				
8. I minimize risks.				
9. I like learning.				
10. I strive for success.				
11. I love, and value the love of others.				
12. I have a circle of good friends.				
13. I stand up for myself.				
14. I make good choices.				
15. I forgive myself if I make mistakes.				
16. I am positive.				
17. I am useful.				
18. I have fun.				
19. I am proud of the things I say and do.				

❷ Be Kind to Others	Strongly Agree	Agree	Disagree	Strongly Disagree
1. I value relationships.				
2. I respect the rights of others.				
3. I am polite and use good manners.				
4. I praise people who do things well.				
5. I work at building and maintaining relationships.				
6. I am tolerant and understanding of difference.				
7. I respect other points of view.				
8. I don't bully or put others down.				
9. I seek a fair chance for all.				
10. I try to manage and resolve conflict.				
11. I cooperate with others.				
12. I support and include others.				
13. I value family life.				
14. I treat others the way they need to be treated.				

"SIX KINDS OF BEST" CHECKLISTS

Name _____

❸ Be Kind to the Environment	Strongly Agree	Agree	Disagree	Strongly Disagree
1. I clean up after myself.				
2. I don't pollute the land, air, or waterways.				
3. I recycle and don't waste.				
4. I don't waste water.				
5. I conserve energy.				
6. I care for natural habitats, wildlife and endangered species.				
7. I use environmentally-friendly products.				
8. I use environmentally-friendly energy sources.				
9. I use resources that can be replaced.				
10. I value our cultural heritage.				

❹ Be the Learning Kind	Strongly Agree	Agree	Disagree	Strongly Disagree
1. I am positive about learning.				
2. I seek knowledge about myself, others and the world around me.				
3. I recognize the value of knowledge.				
4. I have an enquiring mind—I am curious.				
5. I know how I learn best.				
6. I have an open mind.				
7. I am a critical thinker.				
8. I have a global perspective.				
9. I seek learning opportunities everywhere.				
10. I learn from my mistakes.				
11. I am a lifelong learner.				

"SIX KINDS OF BEST" CHECKLISTS

Name _____

❺ Be the Achieving Kind	Strongly Agree	Agree	Disagree	Strongly Disagree
1. I give it a try!				
2. I try lots of different things.				
3. I know what I am good at and enjoy doing.				
4. I do things to the best of my ability.				
5. I pursue quality and personal excellence.				
6. I use my talents.				
7. I have a sense of purpose.				
8. I manage my time effectively.				
9. I manage my money wisely.				
10. I set worthwhile goals and make plans to achieve them.				
11. I am persistent and self-disciplined at achieving my goals.				
12. I look at different ways of doing things.				
13. I have good communication skills.				
14. I have good role models that I look up to.				

❻ Be the Community Kind	Strongly Agree	Agree	Disagree	Strongly Disagree
1. I behave responsibly.				
2. I respect authority.				
3. I follow rules.				
4. I am honest and seek the truth.				
5. I show integrity—I know what is morally and ethically right, and I act that way.				
6. I am useful.				
7. I get involved in the community.				
8. I strive for justice and a "fair chance" for all.				
9. I share with and care for those in need.				
10. I support reconciliation.				
11. I contribute to or support research.				
12. I support freedom.				
13. I strive for peace.				

I am a one of a kind.	Right index finger in the air in front of body.	

1. BE KIND TO YOURSELF

I am kind to myself.	Clenched right fist over heart.	

BE PROUD OF YOUR UNIQUENESS

- Create an individualized name card to attach to your bedroom door or school desk.
- Create an "All About Me" cube. Cut pictures from magazines that relate to things you like and do. Glue them onto a net of a cube made from colored cardboard. Make the cube and hang from the ceiling.
- Write a list of sentences or phrases to reinforce your uniqueness e.g., "I am special because I have freckles across my nose."
- Write rhyming sentences to go with your name.

DEVELOP A SENSE OF IDENTITY

- Create a family mobile. Print the family name (surname) on a rectangular piece of cardboard and hang drawings or paintings of other family members as well as yourself from the card.
- Write a poem about yourself called "Celebrating me!" Complete a sketch or self-portrait to accompany it.
- Design a crest identifying your family.
- Attach a photo of yourself inside a sheet of folded card stock. On the front, give clues about your description, what you like and dislike, what you are good at, etc. See if classmates can guess who is in the card.

KNOW YOUR STRENGTHS AND WORK ON YOUR WEAKNESSES

- Draw a pathway, set of stepping stones, or steps. Write something you are good at at the end or on the final step or stepping stone. Write the steps taken to develop this skill or talent on the other spaces.
- Complete "two stars and a wish" sheets in specific areas; e.g., "I am good at ... and ... but I wish I was better at.... ." These can then be used to assist in goal setting.
- List things you are good at at the top of a picture of a weightlifter lifting a heavy weight and the things you are not so good at underneath the weight.

EXERCISE REGULARLY

- Construct and carry out a weekly diary of regular exercise. Write evaluations at the end of the week.
- Make up fun exercise routines to popular music.
- Create a list of "fun" physical activities to do outside. For example, plan a treasure hunt for natural objects.
- Choose favorite songs to work out exercise routines for the class to perform daily.
- Using pictures in magazines, create a mural of physical activities suitable for young students to participate in.

EAT WELL

- Write details for a healthy day's eating or a weekly menu.
- Collect a healthy recipe from home to bring to school to contribute to a class recipe book of healthy food.
- Create a junk food collage and a health food collage using the brand names from labels on food packaging.
- Make a chart of healthy foods from each food group to incorporate into a weekly eating plan.
- Locate individual food names in a word search. List them under healthy and unhealthy food headings.

SLEEP WELL

- Compose a lullaby or story to read to a younger child before going to sleep.
- Discuss strategies people use when having difficulty getting to sleep; e.g., counting sheep, listening to relaxing music.

TAKE TIME TO RELAX

- Participate in "cool down" exercises such as stretches after break times.
- Build up a library of favorite books to read, music to listen to and games to play.
- Compose and record a piece of soothing music using a variety of musical instruments.
- Follow visual instructions for yoga poses.
- Sit relaxed in a circle of four or five classmates and take turns to tell each other a riddle or joke.

MINIMIZE RISKS

- Identify unsafe practices in the school playground and suggest steps to correct them.
- Create posters that include pictures of ways we can stay safe in different environments.
- Discuss some of the dangers of playing near or in the water, and compile a list of "do's and don't's" to keep children safe.

KEEP LEARNING AND GROWING

- Paint the trunk and branches of a tree on butcher paper (about the size of a door). Attach to a door or wall. Trace around a student's hand and photocopy onto shades of green paper. When a student achieves a personal target at school (such as learning times tables or showing sportsmanship), ask him or her to describe the achievement and write it on a green hand (a leaf). Pin the leaf to the "Achievement tree."
- Encourage students to contribute to a "Stepping Stones to Knowledge" board by writing interesting information they have learned at home on a stone shape and adding it to the board for others to learn and remember.

STRIVE FOR SUCCESS

- Find the meaning of the word "success" in the dictionary and then write sentences which tell what success means to you.
- In groups, write lists of activities on starburst shapes that provide you with "ego food." Spread them upside down on the ground, take turns choosing a starburst and mime or talk about them.
- Set an achievable, specific goal for the class each day. Students should evaluate their success at the end of the day and then reset or change the goal for the following day.

LOVE, AND VALUE THE LOVE OF OTHERS

- Write a poem or simple book which tells why you love members of your family.
- Choose two people who love you. How do you know they love you? Make a list of the things each person does or says to let you know you are loved.
- Make an "I love you … because" card, with a name in the title and an illustration on the front. List five reasons on the inside of the card and give it to someone special.

DEVELOP A CIRCLE OF GOOD FRIENDS

- Design a poster of words which show what a good friend is like; e.g., loyal, friendly, supportive, etc.
- Write a poem in the shape of a circle about what makes a quality friend.
- Use a "Y-Chart" to record student ideas about what good friends look like (friendly, kind, smiling), sound like (laughing, "Play with me," "Can I help you?") and feel like (happy, good, fun).

STAND UP FOR YOURSELF

- Listen to scenarios and practice showing assertiveness in those situations which need it.
- It can take a lot of confidence and courage to stand up for yourself. Work with a small group to make up a role-play about someone being bullied. Show how this person solved the problem and stood up for himself or herself.
- Role play peer pressure scenarios where one child is being pressured into doing something he or she knows is wrong.

MAKE GOOD CHOICES

- Play a game of hopscotch where each square has a good and bad choice option to choose.
- Discuss good and bad food choices and safe places to play.

FORGIVE YOURSELF IF YOU MAKE MISTAKES

- Design merit certificates for forgiving yourself for making a mistake, for not being afraid to make a mistake and learning by making a mistake.

- If you did something really bad and you felt terrible about it, what could you do to make yourself feel better (e.g., say sorry or try to fix your mistakes)? How could other people help you to feel better about it?

BE POSITIVE

- Make a list of positive words, phrases and actions such as "Greet people with a smile," "Speak clearly," "Hold your head high." Write in colorful script on a large sheet of paper to create an attractive poster to motivate other students.
- Create an "I feel great when …" poster of a happy face. Students should write their ideas on smiling mouth shapes to be added to the poster.

BE USEFUL

- Complete a diary of chores done at school and home for a week.
- Look around at home for things that you could do to help your parents; e.g., collecting the newspapers on recycling day, emptying the lunch boxes after school, bringing toys in from the yard at the end of the day.
- Discuss the people class members enjoy helping, what they do to help and why they feel good about it.

HAVE SOME FUN

- Write "knock-knock" jokes or riddles to tell at a given time at the end of the day.
- Think about a character in a book, movie, or on television who has a fun life. Make a list of the fun things he or she does. Check the ones you would like to do.

BE PROUD OF THE THINGS YOU SAY AND DO

- Role-play using courteous language for selected situations such as meeting a new person or accidentally running into someone in the playground.
- Draw one smiling face and one sad face. During the day, tally the number of times you make someone happy or sad by the things you say. Draw the tally marks as strands of hair on each face. At the end of the day, which face has more hair? Share your results with the class.
- Glue a photo of yourself onto white card stock. Around the photo, paint the outline of different colored balloons and gold and silver stars. In each one, write something about yourself that makes you feel proud about who you are. Display.
- Students work in pairs and take turns to say nice things about each other. They choose the comment they liked best and repeat it to the class, explaining why it made them feel good.

INTRODUCTION

Often students are told to be nice to other people, but how often are they told to be kind to themselves? All people, at times, feel bad about themselves or put themselves "down." In fact, we are often harsher critics of ourselves than others are. It is really important to encourage students to think positively about themselves as much as possible to develop high self-esteem — to "be kind to yourself."

Worksheet Information

Page 24 – Be Proud of Your Uniqueness
- Discuss why each of us is unique and listen to selected students tell why they are unique.
- Complete the activity as directed on the worksheet, then allow some students to read their poems to the class.

Page 25 – Develop a Sense of Identity
- What things are important to you?
- Why are they important?
- What do these things say about us; do they give us a purpose or a sense of identity?

Page 26 – Know Your Strengths and Work on Your Weaknesses
- Discuss and group students by strengths and weaknesses.
- Students should choose two or three strengths or weaknesses to write in the boxes for Question 1. Some discussion about how to improve weaknesses may be needed before completing Question 2.

Page 27 – Exercise Regularly
- Read the information and allow students to complete the worksheet as directed.

Page 28 – Eat Well
- Read the information and allow students to complete the worksheet as directed. The students should share the pictures they drew for Question 3, discussing whether they were made up of more healthy or unhealthy foods.

Page 29 – Sleep Well
- Why is it important to get enough sleep?
- How much sleep does someone your age need each night?
- How do you feel when you wake up in the morning?

Page 30 – Take Time to Relax
- Why is it important to take time to relax?
- What do you do to relax?
- Does relaxing mean you have to sit quietly?

Page 31 – Minimize Risks
- Why do we have safety rules?
- What things do you do to stay safe at school? At home? Going to and from school? At the beach? At the park?

Page 32 – Keep Learning and Growing
- What kind of things could you do as a baby? At one? At two?, etc.
- Do you think there is a time when you will stop learning how to do things? Why?/Why not?
- Who helps you to learn to do things? (themselves, teachers, parents, etc.)

Page 33 – Strive for Success
- Students cut out the template on the page and fold to form a four-page booklet. They complete the activity by drawing appropriate pictures and/or writing words for each page.
- What are some things you are good at?
- Is everyone good at the same things?
- How do you feel when you are doing something you are good at?

Page 34 – Love, and Value the Love of Others
- How do you show your family that you love them?
- How do you know they love you?
- If your mom, dad, etc., is angry with you, does that mean they don't love you?

Page 35 – Develop a Circle of Good Friends
- Who is a good friend of yours?
- Why is this person a good friend?
- Are you a good friend?

Page 36 – Stand Up for Yourself
- Have you ever been asked to do something that you didn't feel like doing or you knew was wrong?
- Do you find it hard to say "no" to your friends?
- Why is it important to stand up for yourself?

Page 37 – Make Good Choices
- Enlarge the worksheet (optional) and cut out cards. They can be given to students to read and make choices individually, in pairs, in small groups or as a whole class. Discuss choice consequences.
- What are some choices you have to make each day?
- How do you know if they are good or bad choices?
- How do you feel when you make: the right·choice? The wrong choice?

Page 38 – Forgive Yourself If You Make Mistakes

- Read and discuss the story of "The Ant and the Grasshopper" with the students. Discuss how the grasshopper realized his mistake by not storing food for winter as he wanted to play. Students write an ending to the story in their own words to show the grasshopper forgave himself and what he did to rectify the situation and learn from it.
- How do you feel when you make a mistake?
- How should you feel when you make a mistake?

Page 39 – Be Positive

- What does being positive mean?
- How do you know if someone is feeling positive?
- What does "Think up, not down" mean?

Page 40 – Be Useful

- What does being useful mean?
- How are you useful?
- How does being useful make you feel?

Page 41 – Have Some Fun

- What are some of the things you do to have fun?
- What makes you laugh?
- How does laughing make you feel?

Page 42 – Be Proud of the Things You Say and Do

- What are some things people do that they would probably feel proud about?
- How would you know if someone was feeling proud? What might they say or do?
- Why do you think people say, "He was as proud as a peacock"?

Answers

page 29

2. (a) Red – grumpy, can't be bothered, sad, yawn a lot, tired, sick, can't concentrate, make mistakes in schoolwork, rub eyes, no energy, upset, slow to do things

   (b) Green – happy, smile a lot, lots of energy, laugh, quick to answer questions, friendly

Graphic Organizer Example

T-Chart

Same	Different

The One and Only!

1. Read the poem.

> *I am special. I am unique.*
>
> *You won't find another, no matter how hard you seek.*
>
> *I'm not like you. You're not like me.*
>
> *But it keeps life interesting, as you will see!*

2. Use the dictionary to write the meaning of the word *unique*.

_____

_____

_____

3. Write words and phrases which tell why you are
   unique; e.g., freckled, friendly, a good joke teller, etc.

4. Use some of the words above to write an acrostic poem about
   yourself telling why you are unique.

U _____

N _____

I _____

Q _____

U _____

E _____

Identity Badge

An identity badge is a card which tells about the person carrying the card in their purse, wallet, or bag. In some countries, people must carry them with them all the time to show that they live in that country.

Name: Mortimer Singh
Address: Leafy Lane Terrace
Brightonville WA 98760
Licensed to use:
rollerblades, racing bike, surfboard
go-kart, snowboard, windsurfer

478 219 660 598 000 - 1

Answer the questions below to help you design an identity badge for yourself.

1. Color the shape you would like your identity badge to be.

 circle   rectangle   star   other _____

2. Write the information which you would want to include on your identity badge.

_____

_____

_____

3. Write the colors which you would like to have on your identity badge and what those colors will be used for. For example, black for the printing, gold for the border, etc.

Color	Where/What

4. Draw your completed identity badge.

Balance the Scales

1. Write words to show what you are good at (strengths) and what you need to improve (weaknesses) above each of the headings.

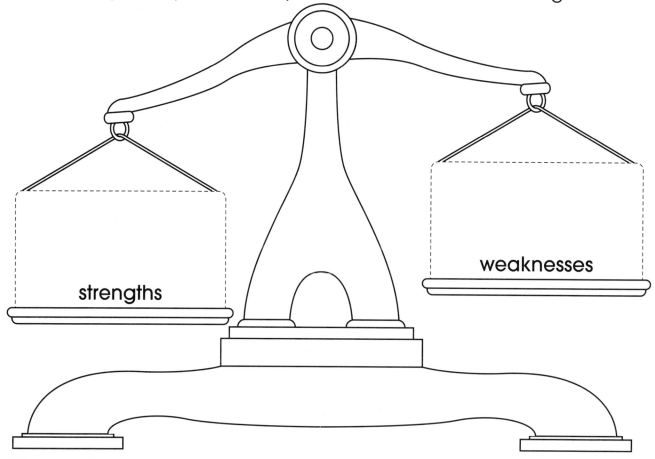

strengths

weaknesses

2. Choose four weaknesses and write one way to improve each.

Weakness	Way to Improve It
(a)	
(b)	
(c)	
(d)	

26

Fun Exercise

Exercise is an important part of keeping healthy and fit.

1. Circle the forms of exercise which you do on a regular basis.

running	skipping	hopping	jumping	playing outside
swimming	dancing	gymnastics	soccer	baseball
walking	climbing	volleyball	tennis	ballet

2. Write or draw some others you may do that are not on the list above (if you have any!).

Often we exercise without realizing it. We call this "incidental movement." This may include things like getting up to change the television channel without using the remote control, walking to school, or bike riding with a friend.

3. In the boxes, write three more ways you could add more "incidental movement" to your day. One has been done for you. You may discuss these with a partner.

Dance with your favorite music video clip when it comes on the television	

4. Think of a really fun exercise activity which you have not tried before but would love to try. Write it below.

You Are What You Eat!

Our bodies need healthy food to stay well. It is okay to have unhealthy food occasionally as "treats," but most of the time it is better to eat a healthy diet.

1. Check the healthy foods which you eat or drink regularly.

   bread ❏   cereal ❏

   rice ❏   pasta ❏

   vegetables ❏   fish ❏

   meat ❏   eggs ❏

   cheese ❏   yogurt ❏

   fruit ❏   milk ❏

   water ❏   legumes ❏

   chicken ❏   nuts ❏

2. Draw and label food in the boxes. Check to show if they are healthy or unhealthy

   My Favorite "Takeout" Meal

   healthy ❏   unhealthy ❏

   My Favorite Treat

   healthy ❏   unhealthy ❏

3. If our bodies were made up of the types of food which we like to eat, what would we look like?

   Draw a "food" person picture of yourself.

28

A Good Night's Sleep

*Look at the two children below. One is yawning because she **didn't** have a good night's sleep. The other is bright and cheery because he **did** have a good night's sleep.*

1. Write what you think each child might be thinking in the thought bubbles.

2. (a) Color the boxes red that describe how people might act or feel if they **have not** had enough sleep.

   (b) Color the boxes green that describe how people might act or feel if they **have** had enough sleep.

grumpy	happy	can't be bothered	sad	yawn a lot	tired
smile a lot	lots of energy	sick	can't concentrate	laugh	make mistakes in school work
rub eyes	no energy	upset	quick to answer questions	slow to do things	friendly

Ways to Relax

1. Use the ideas below to survey your class to find their favorite ways to relax.

2. Add two more ideas, if necessary.

3. Graph the results.

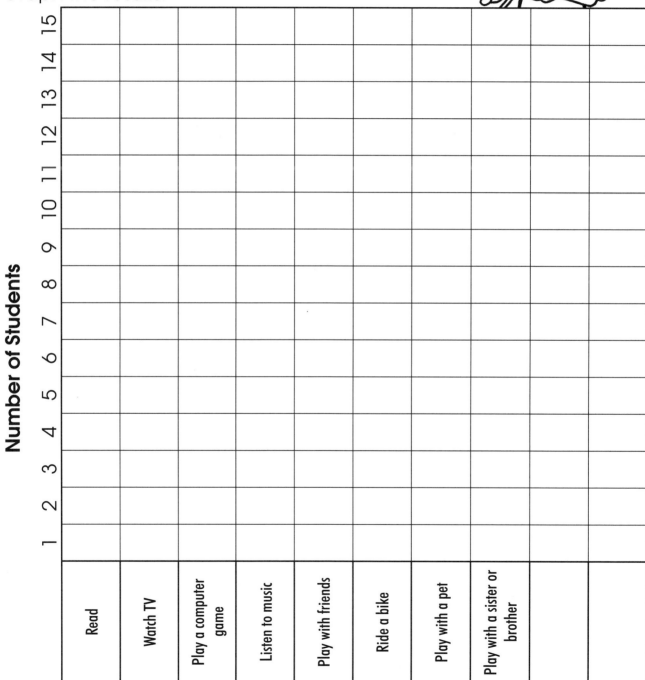

Number of Students

15 14 13 12 11 10 9 8 7 6 5 4 3 2 1

Read | Watch TV | Play a computer game | Listen to music | Play with friends | Ride a bike | Play with a pet | Play with a sister or brother

Ways to Relax

Ways to Stay Safe

Color the pictures, then cut out the sentences and glue them under the correct pictures.

Cross the road carefully.	Always wear a helmet.
Remember to wear sunscreen and a hat.	Don't play with matches.
Swim between the flags at the beach.	Know how deep the water is before jumping or diving in.

Then and Now

As you get older, there are more and more things you learn to do.

Write words and/or draw pictures to show how you did the things below when you were about three years old and how you do them now.

	Three	Now
Dressing		
Eating		
Talking		
Counting		
Reading		
Playing		

32

I'm a Star!

THE THING I
DO BEST ...

MY BEST QUALITY ...

I'M A STAR!

MY PROUDEST
MOMENT ...

by _____

33

"I Love You" Cookies

Follow the recipe for making the heart-shaped cookies below. Give one to each family member or person you love with a hug, kiss and/or an "I love you."

You will need:
- 1 cup butter
- 1 ⅓ cups icing sugar
- 4 cups plain flour
- pink icing
- silver balls or colored sprinkles for decorations
- 4 teaspoons vanilla extract
- 2 egg yolks
- rolling pin, sifter and bowl
- heart-shaped cutters

SCRUMPO professional

 325 °F

1. Preheat the oven to 325 °F. Mix butter, egg yolks, icing sugar and vanilla in a bowl.

2. Sift flour into the mixture and mix well.

3. Roll out thinly with a rolling pin. Place in fridge until firm.

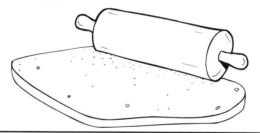

4. Cut the dough mixture into heart shapes. Bake in oven for 15 minutes.

5. Leave on oven tray for five minutes. Then place on a wire rack to cool.

6. Spread icing onto cookies. Decorate with silver balls or colored sprinkles.

34

What Makes a Good Friend?

Everyone needs to have friends. Good friends are fun to be with and share things with you.

1. (a) Color the words and phrases below that describe a good friend.

   (b) Add more of your own in the letter "D."

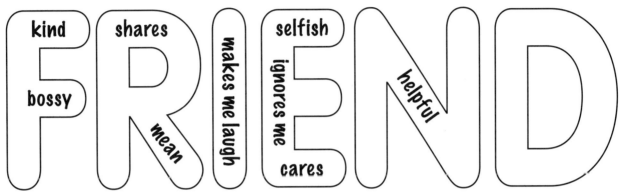

2. (a) Write the names of some of your good friends in the border of the "friend oval."

   (b) Draw a picture of you playing with a friend or friends in the middle.

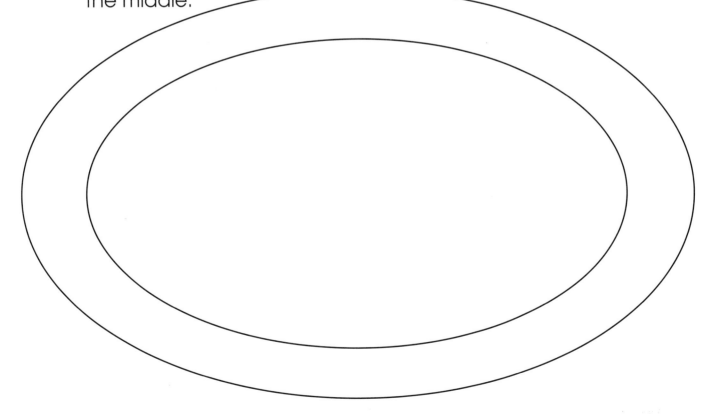

Think For Yourself

It is important to think for yourself and make up your mind about what to do. Sometimes the people you are with want to do something that you don't feel like doing or you know is wrong. Stand up for yourself and say you don't want to.

1. Look at the pictures below. Each one shows someone who doesn't want to do what the others are going to do. In the speech bubbles, write what each person could say.

36

What Would You Choose to Do?

Your mom has put some things on the kitchen counter for you to put in your lunch box to eat at snack time. You can choose two things. Circle them.

package of chips   banana
granola bar   tub of yogurt
candy   apple
strawberries   chocolate bar

Your friend suggests that you both take a short cut home from school and walk through the field.

What do you choose to do?

You and your sister are dancing to music in the family room when you bang into the bookshelf. A statue falls off and breaks.

What do you choose to do?

Your class is having a spelling test. The person who sits next to you has not covered his words up and you can see them.

What do you choose to do?

You and a friend are walking past the school cafeteria when you see a $5 bill on the ground.

What do you choose to do?

The football you are kicking with friends lands on the roof.

What do you choose to do?

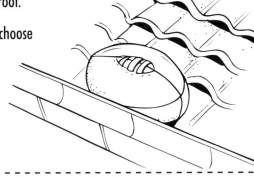

You are playing a game with some classmates and see another classmate watching as if he or she wants to join in.

What do you choose to do?

You and a friend are eating lunch. Your friend suggests you both leave your trash on the ground as the trashcan is on the other side of the lunch area.

What do you choose to do?

The Ant and the Grasshopper

One warm summer's day, a grasshopper was happily chirping about in a cornfield. Suddenly, he noticed an ant making his way back to his nest with an ear of corn.

"What are you doing with the corn?" he asked.

"I'm storing it for winter," replied the ant.

"Why worry about winter now?" said the grasshopper.

"Come and play with me. It's such a lovely day!"

But the ant kept working. Time and time again he struggled past the grasshopper with ears of corn. He gathered food all through summer and into autumn. The grasshopper kept chirping and hopping and playing.

Winter came. There was no food to be found on the ground or on the bare plants. The grasshopper grew hungry and became weaker and weaker. He watched the ants distributing food from their store ...

Write an ending for the story in your own words.

_____

_____

_____

_____

_____

_____

_____

Positive Pete and Negative Ned

1. (a) Read what the boys said and draw a line from each phrase to the boy you think said it.

Great idea!
Let's do it!
No way!
I'll try again.
Go away!
It's too hard.
How boring!
Get lost!
Come on!
How interesting!
Yuk!
I don't want to.
I like it!
You're great!
This is fun!
This rocks!
I can do it!
Don't give up!
How stupid!
I give up.
Wow!

Ned

Pete

(b) Which boy do you think is happier? _____

(c) Who would you rather play with? _____

Why?_____

_____

2. Write two positive things you like to say or hear someone say to you.

| |
| |

I'm Useful

We can all be useful by making and doing things and helping other people.

1. Who do you help?

   (a) At school I help _____ when I

   _____ .

   (b) At home I help _____ when I

   _____ .

2. What can you make? Draw a picture and complete the sentence.

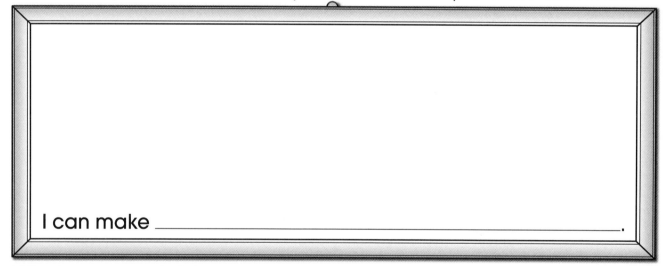

   I can make _____ .

3. What can you do? Draw a picture and complete the sentence.

   I can _____ .

40

Having Fun

1. (a) Draw two pictures showing you doing a fun thing. Describe what it is that you are doing that is fun.

 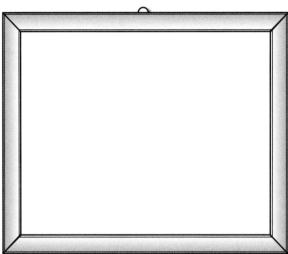

_____ is fun.   _____ is fun.

2. (a) Read the riddles.

> **What is black and white and read all over?**
> A newspaper
>
> **Why did the elephant paint his toenails red?**
> So he could hide in the strawberry patch

(b) Did you enjoy them?

_____

3. (a) Read the jokes.

> **What is a frog's favorite candy?**
> A lolli-hop
>
> **How do fish get to school?**
> By octobus

(b) Are they funny?

_____

3. Write a joke or a riddle for others to enjoy.

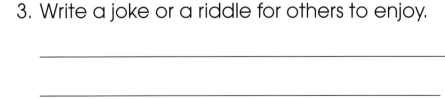

I'm Great

1. Think about something you did that you feel proud of. Make a merit certificate to award to yourself. Draw a picture and tell what you did.

Merit Certificate

This merit certificate is awarded to

_____

for: _____

_____

_____

Date: _____   Signature: _____

2. BE KIND TO OTHERS

THE SIX KINDS OF BEST

KIND TO OTHERS

KIND TO THE ENVIRONMENT

KIND TO YOURSELF

BE

KIND THE LEARNING

KIND THE ACHIEVING

KIND THE COMMUNITY

VALUES EDUCATION PROGRAM

I am kind to others.	From clenched fist over heart, swing right arm clockwise and point out-wards.	

VALUE RELATIONSHIPS

- Discuss why grandparents are special, the things they say and do, and what they enjoy. Invite grandparents to a morning or afternoon tea and entertain them.
- Use visual aids to create diagrams of different relationships you have with people in your lives; e.g., sister, friend, student, grandparent, sports coach.
- Make simple gifts to show others how much you appreciate them.

RESPECT THE RIGHTS OF OTHERS

- Perform role-plays where children are not respecting the rights of others; e.g., talking in school instead of listening to the teacher, taking someone's colored pencil without asking. Then role-play the correct way to behave.
- Everyone has rights . One of these rights is to be safe at school. Discuss what we all have to do to make sure everyone has this right.
- Construct two lists—one which details student rights and one which gives information about responsibilities.

BE POLITE AND USE GOOD MANNERS

- Concentrate on remembering to use one particular aspect of good manners in your class each week; e.g., saying "Excuse me" before interrupting a conversation.
- Use puppets to role-play scenarios demonstrating either good or bad manners; e.g., shopping or answering the telephone. Encourage students to comment on the manners demonstrated.
- Write rhymes which tell how to use the correct manners in different situations. Example: When I was walking down the street, I saw a friend I've yet to meet. I said, "Hello! Good morning to you!" He said, "Good day! Nice to meet you too!"

PRAISE PEOPLE WHO DO THINGS WELL

- Each day students nominate others who have done something well. They should give reasons for their nomination, and if their nominee is accepted, that child's name is written in a star shape and displayed.
- Keep a written record of nice comments given and the person who gave them in class for a week. Tally the results and present the person with the highest score a specially decorated certificate.

DEVELOP GOOD PEOPLE SKILLS

- Practice the correct way to introduce someone and then "introduce" a class member to others as if meeting him/her for the first time, making him/her feel welcome.
- Draw smiles on a variety of people's faces with a label that says "A smile brightens up everyone's day."
- Discuss why good manners are important if we want to get along well with others, and make lists of good and bad manners that help our relationships.

- Think of a compliment to give to a different class member each day until all have been given a compliment. Repeat, finding two compliments for two different class members each day, and so on.

WORK AT BUILDING AND MAINTAINING RELATIONSHIPS

- Read or listen to a story such as *Charlotte's Web* by E.B. White that highlights the building of a wonderful friendship—in this story between Charlotte, the spider, and Wilbur, the pig.
- Discuss some of the ways we let people know that we like them.
- Draw a collection of faces that are important to you. Under each face, write two suggestions for something nice you can do for that person. Display it where you can remind yourself to do it.

BE TOLERANT AND UNDERSTANDING OF DIFFERENCE

- Create a mural of pictures from magazines of people of different ages and nationalities. List words and phrases to identify how people can be different physically; e.g., freckled, olive-skinned, young, old, tall, wear glasses.
- Read the story of "The Ugly Ducking" and discuss why the "duckling" was rejected by the others and if people also do this to those who look different.
- Invite a disabled child (or group of children) into the room for a "play" session. Discuss any difficulties encountered. Repeat by visiting them in their school or classroom and compare experiences.

RESPECT OTHER POINTS OF VIEW

- Students take turns in picking questions written on folded slips of paper out of a container. After a minute to think of a reply, the student reads out the question and states his or her point of view to the class or small group. Others can then say whether they agree or not. Sample questions could be: Do you think children should make their own bed? Do you think ketchup is good on steak?
- Students work in pairs and interview each other, asking a set of yes/no questions to determine their partner's point of view about a number of issues. They compare their answers and tally the questions on which they agree and those they don't. Students should understand that there is no right or wrong answer and that everyone is entitled to his or her opinion.
- Interview other class members about their likes, dislikes, hobbies, favorite television programs, favorite books, etc., and compare.

DON'T BULLY OR PUT OTHERS DOWN

- View an illustrated scenario with text in speech bubbles of a bullying situation. Color the pictures, then cut out and sequence correctly. Discuss what is happening, how the characters feel and what could be done about it.
- Students draw a cartoon strip showing someone being bullied and what happened about it. They should include speech bubbles.
- Write a list of assertive phrases for students to practice. Display on a chart.
- Compose charts for students to use as motivation (or to simplify the steps to take) in a bullying situation; for example, "Just say"; "No"; "then"; "Go, Go, Go!"

SEEK A FAIR CHANCE FOR ALL

- Role-play a situation where a group of students are playing a game and one notices another student watching and wishing he or she could join in the game. All characters could portray positive and negative behavior, but in the end, a fair chance is achieved.
- Students work in groups of three or four to discuss things they think are not fair in a specific category; e.g., in their classroom, in their family, in sports, in underdeveloped countries. They then share their ideas with the class.
- Carry out group activities with each student having a chance to be leader, recorder, or scribe, as dictated by the activity.

MANAGE AND RESOLVE CONFLICT

- In the center of a picture of a pot boiling over or a kettle boiling, briefly describe a situation that makes you mad. Underneath, complete a sentence about what you should and shouldn't do in this situation.
- Discuss why the concept "Don't get mad, get even" often escalates conflict and is not the best way to resolve it. Pose scenarios and have students suggest some alternative conflict resolutions.
- Read and explain the steps to resolving conflict—What is the problem? How do you feel? How can we fix the problem? Brainstorm ways to fix the problem. Choose the best option. Agree on the final solution. Reinforce on a regular basis in the classroom and playground.

COOPERATE AND BE A TEAM PLAYER

- Groups of students are given the same set of instructions for completing a task together; e.g., a craft activity such as constructing an object out of recycled materials. When complete, students compare their end results and fill in an evaluation about how well they worked as a team.
- Conduct small group discussions to compile a class list of the qualities of a great team member.

- List groups which make a team; e.g., different types of sporting teams, teams of animals, debating teams, etc. Students choose a favorite sporting team and construct a poster using team colors for headings or decorations, newspaper/magazine clippings or drawings of players. Display with sentences which tell why the team performs well together.

SUPPORT AND INCLUDE OTHERS

- Devise a cartoon strip where a human, animal, or imaginary character is at first left out of a group, but ends up being included.
- Discuss the things people say when they don't want you to play with them and how it makes you feel. Make a list of what they could say instead to make you feel welcome.
- Write a story about a child who is excluded from a group, but carries out a heroic act and becomes popular with everyone.
- Read the story of "The Ugly Duckling" and discuss how he was shunned by the beautiful swans at first, but was included once he changed into a swan.

VALUE FAMILY LIFE

- Create a poem about what your family means to you to frame and display at home.
- Create a collage of illustrations, photographs and written descriptions about "Things Our Families Do."
- Create "vouchers" for helpful things which can be redeemed by family members.

TREAT OTHERS THE WAY THEY NEED TO BE TREATED

- Read the story of "The Elves and the Shoemaker" to highlight how we should treat others the way they need to be treated.
- Discuss Goldilocks' behavior at the three bears' house and if the three bears deserved to be treated that way. Retell the story differently.
- Write about two different things you could do to make a sad person happy.
- Role-play a variety of situations which show correct and incorrect ways of treating:
    - An old person in a very crowded street.
    - A mother with a baby and a little child standing on a crowded bus.
    - A person carrying two large bags of groceries to his/her car.
    - A lonely old man in a retirement home.

Introduction

Being kind to others is an essential element in the development of good people skills. These skills are important in forming and maintaining the many different relationships which are an integral part of living in society. Students need to understand the nature and importance of relationships and how to form and support them. Comprehending and considering the needs of others and knowing how to interact with them in a positive way are the keys to good relationships.

Worksheet Information

Page 48 – Value Relationships

- What does the word "relationship" mean?
- Who are some people you have a good relationship with?
- How do you show these people you care about them?

Page 49 – Respect the Rights of Others

- What does "respect" mean? How can we show respect?
- What does "courtesy" mean? How can we show courtesy?
- What are some things you will find in a safe, clean environment?

Page 50 – Be Polite and Use Good Manners

- What are some things a person would do and say to show he or she has good manners?
- What are some things a person would do and say to show he or she has bad manners?
- What manners do you do well?

Page 51 – Praise People Who Do Things Well

- Discuss with the students that if they notice someone has done something well, it is really nice to let him or her know. It not only makes that person feel good, but makes the giver get a "warm fuzzy" inside as well!
- Students choose an appropriate shape for someone at home or school who has done something well. They cut it out, write a message on it, decorate it and give it to the person saying "Well done!"
- Other suggestions: The page could be enlarged; the shapes could be glued onto the front of a folded piece of card stock to make a personalized card; a hole could be made with a paper punch at the top of the shape and yarn or curling ribbon threaded through to hang for display.

Page 52 – Develop Good People Skills

- What does having "good people skills" mean?
- Why do we need good people skills?
- What good people skills do you have?

Page 53 – Work at Building and Maintaining Relationships

- Complete the worksheet as directed. Selected students may read their letters to the class. If possible, letters may be placed in an envelope, addressed and mailed.

Page 54 – Be Tolerant and Understanding of Difference

- Discuss where the parents of different students may have come from. Talk about interesting customs, language or habits.
- Encourage students when drawing faces to put in all the lines and shapes they can see.

Page 55 – Respect Other Points of View

- Discuss the activity with the students so they understand completely what is to be done. Form pairs, complete the first column, then swap partners with another pair until three people have been interviewed. Discuss what was discovered as a class.

Page 56 – Don't Bully or Put Others Down

- What is bullying and what types of bullying are there?
- Read and discuss the poem with the students first, then read the information. Form pairs to share information for Question 2.
- Discuss the scenarios and possible replies.
- Complete Question 4 as directed.

Page 57 – Seek a Fair Chance for All

- Explain the various parts of a narrative. Discuss possible storylines as suggested by the students. If possible, model planning and writing an example for the students.

Page 58 – Manage and Resolve Conflict

- Discuss what a conflict is and the steps given to resolve a conflict. Students complete the worksheet as directed. Students should not feel compelled to write about a conflict which may be unsettling to them.

Page 59 – Cooperate and Be a Team Player

- Students should complete this activity as a team to find out how well they can work together. Students should complete the activity as directed on the worksheet.

Page 60 – Support and Include Others

- The students should make the cube as directed on the worksheet. Students may take turns to throw the cube and think of a scenario to match the writing on the card. For example, asking "Would you like to join in our game?" would be an appropriate action in response to a scenario where a child is sitting on his/her own in the playground or is new to the school. Teachers may suggest possible scenarios before students throw the cube and try to think of scenarios of their own.

Page 61 – *Value Family Life*

- Students fill out the vouchers with special things they would do. For example, take out the trash for a week, collect the mail, walk the dog for three days, help to hang out the clothes, or wash the car.

Page 62 – *Treat Others the Way They Need to Be Treated*

- Read the fable with the students and discuss what a moral is and what this particular one means. Students complete the worksheet as directed, then discuss their answers to Question 3.

Answers

Page 52:

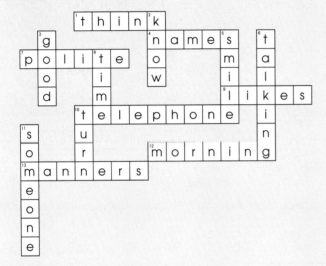

Graphic Organizer Example

Senses Chart

Looks	
Tastes	
Feels	
Smells	
Sounds	

5W Chart

Who	
What	
Where	
When	
Why	

People I Care About

There are many people in your life whom you care about and who care about you. You will feel closer to some of these people than others. This means you have a closer relationship.

1. Write your name under the box in the middle of the page. Draw your face in the box.

2. Choose four people with whom you have a close relationship. Write a name in each box, draw his/her face and write a sentence about him/her.

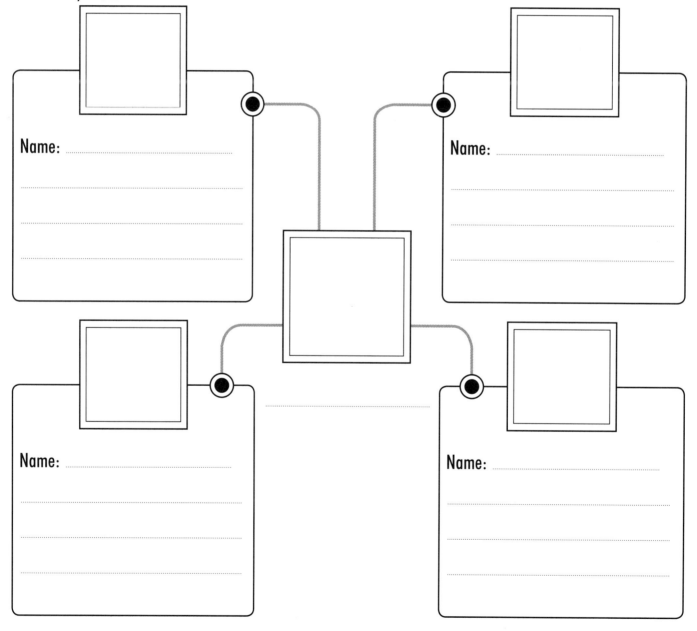

Name:

Name:

Name:

Name:

48

We All Have Rights

Everyone has the right to be treated with courtesy and respect and to work in a safe, clean environment.

Read about some of the ways we can do this at home, at school and in the community. Add more ways under each heading.

	Courtesy and Respect	Stay Safe	Stay Clean
At Home			• Help to load the dishwasher.
At School		• Use the school crossing to cross the road.	
In the Community	• Don't push people around when using playground equipment.		

Using Good Manners

If everyone used good manners all the time, what a happy place the world would be to live in! Good manners means saying words such as "please," "thank you" and "excuse me" at the right times. It also means doing things like waiting your turn and asking before using something.

Look at the pictures below. Write what the people could be saying to each other. Remember to use "good manners" words.

50

Well Done!

51

Good People Skills Crossword

Complete the crossword below. All the clues will give you lots of ideas for having good people skills, which make it easy to get along with others.

ACROSS

1. Listen to other people's opinions. They may not _____ the same way as you.
4. Use the _____ of people when you speak to them.
7. Another word for "courteous" is _____.
9. Everyone _____ a well-mannered person.
10. Answer the _____ correctly.
12. Use greetings such as "Good _____," "Hello," "Hi" and "See you."
13. Good _____ are important.

DOWN

2. Nod or smile back to people you _____.
3. A polite greeting is "_____ morning."
5. A _____ brightens everyone's day.
6. Look at people who are _____ to you.
8. Be on _____.
10. Wait for your _____.
11. Say "Excuse me" if you need to interrupt _____ who is speaking to another person.

Letter to an Important Person

1. Answer the questions.

    (a) Who are the most important people to you?

    _____

    (b) Why are they important to you?

    _____

    _____

    _____

    (c) What things could you do to show that them that they are important to you?

    _____

    _____

2. Choose one of the people to write a letter to. Include some of the information in the answers to the questions above.

Dear ....

....

....

....

....

....

....

....

....

Love from ....

Lots of Different People

Our country is made up of people from many different backgrounds. Some people have parents who were born in another country, some may speak other languages, some practice different religions and some may look different from you. We come in all different shapes and sizes. We have different likes and dislikes. This makes our country an interesting place in which to live.

1. Find four class members who look very different from each other and draw their faces in the shapes below. Color them using the correct colors. Label each face with the person's name.

2. Write or tell a story about an imaginary country where everyone looks the same, thinks the same and does the same thing. Mention the problems in living in such a country.

What Do You Think?

1. Use the table below to interview three classmates and write what they think about the topics given.

Topic	Name of Classmate	Name of Classmate	Name of Classmate
(a) We should plant trees from all over the world in the school playground.			
(b) Boys and girls should go to different schools.			
(c) Children use computers too much.			
(d) Animals should never be kept in zoos.			

Brothers and Sisters

1. Read the poem.

My brother Mark is bigger than me.

He wrestles with me and likes to tease.

When Mark hurts me, I tell my Dad.

He makes him stop "cause he's been bad!"

My sister Meg is such a pest.

She borrows some toys and breaks the rest.

But when I call her "baby" or "short stuff,"

Dad says to me, "That's enough!"

Other people can be hurt if we punch, kick, or hit them, but they can also be hurt by the mean things we say to them.

2. Find a partner and tell them about a time when someone said something mean to you and how you felt about it.

3. Read the scenarios below and write a good reply.

(a) Trudy is wearing her new school shoes and feeling very fashionable.

Jackie says, "Don't you know that nobody wears those shoes any more! You are so not 'cool'!"

What could Trudy say? _____

_____

(b) David is choosing other boys to play on the football team.

"I can't choose you, Glen!" says David. " You're a hopeless player!"

What could Glen say? _____

_____

4. On the back of the worksheet, write sentences to make others feel good about themselves.

Fair Chance! Narrative Plan

1. Plan a narrative about an animal who cheated in the annual Jungle Gymbaroo. (He did not give the others a fair chance!)

Title	
Orientation When? Where? Who?	
Complication What was the problem?	
Events What happened?	
Resolution How was the problem fixed?	
Ending	

2. Write your narrative on a separate sheet of paper.

Fixing a Conflict Problem

Conflict happens when people disagree about something. There are simple steps which people can use to try to fix a conflict.

1. Read the steps.

   (a) Stop and cool off.

   (b) Decide what the problem is and say how you feel.

   (c) Decide what needs to be done to fix the problem.

   (d) Think of some ways to fix the problem.

   (e) Choose the way that suits everyone the best.

   (f) Agree on the best way to fix the problem.

2. Write about a conflict you may have had with a friend or family member.

3. Use the steps to show ways to fix the problem.

(a) Stop and cool off.	
(b) What was the problem and how did you feel?	
(c) What needed to be done to fix the problem?	
(d) What were some ways to fix it?	
(e) Circle the best way to fix it.	
(f) Agree on the best way to fix the problem.	

58

Environmental Team

When people work together (cooperate), they can do amazing things!

Your task is to develop a plan for an area of the playground which needs improvement.

1. Form a group of four and write the names of the team members.

   _____

2. List two possible problem areas and ways to improve them.

   • _____

   _____

   • _____

   _____

3. Discuss them and choose one to write below.

   "Our chosen area is _____

   and we plan to improve it by _____

   _____."

4. Draw a plan of your idea.

   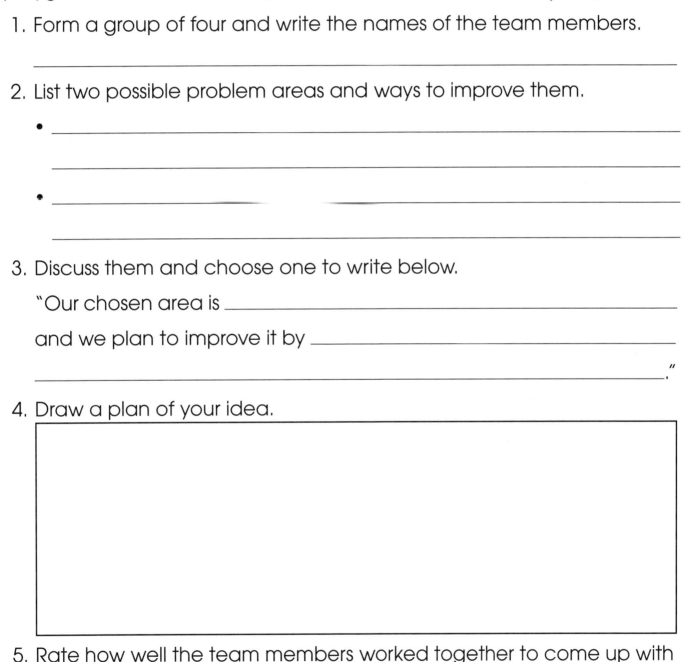

5. Rate how well the team members worked together to come up with a plan. Circle the most appropriate word or words.

   Hopeless!   **Not well!**   **Okay!**   **Great!**   **Fantastic!**

"Supporting and Including Others" Cube

1. Color, cut and paste the cube.

2. Carefully roll the cube.

3. Read the method used to show support or to include others.

4. Give a simple scenario to tell when you would use this method.

Listen as they share their feelings with you.

Clap or cheer loudly as part of the crowd or audience.

Offer something of yours to them to replace the one they lost.

Invite them to your house to play after school or on the weekend.

Ask them if they would like to join in your game.

Say some encouraging words to make them feel better about themselves.

Family Vouchers

Complete the vouchers to *do* something nice for each member of your family to show that you appreciate him/her.

I agree to _____

for _____ because _____

_____

_____

Signed _____

I agree to _____

for _____ because _____

_____

_____

Signed _____

I agree to _____

for _____ because _____

_____

_____

Signed _____

The Fox and the Stork

1. Read the fable.

> **O**nce upon a time, the Fox and the Stork were good friends. They liked visiting each other.
>
> One day, the Fox invited the Stork for dinner. As a joke, he put the soup out in two very shallow bowls. The Fox was easily able to lap up the soup, but the Stork could only get the edge of her long beak into the bowl. She couldn't eat very much. At the end of the meal, she was still feeling hungry.
>
> "I'm sorry that you didn't like the soup," said the Fox.
>
> "That's okay," replied the Stork. "I hope you'll come to my house soon and have dinner with me."
>
> Soon the day arrived for the Fox to visit the Stork for dinner. When they sat down for dinner, there were only two jars with long necks and very narrow mouths on the table. The Stork was easily able to eat her meal, but the Fox could only lick just inside the rim of the jar.
>
> "I'm not sorry about the dinner," said the Stork.
>
> The moral of this fable is: One bad turn deserves another.

2. Did the Stork do the right thing by acting the way she did?

   Yes ❑ No ❑ Why? _____

   _____

3. What could the Fox and the Stork do to treat each other as they need to be treated?

   _____

   _____

   _____

   _____

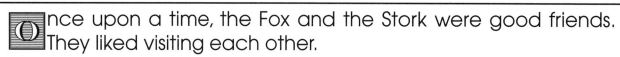

3. BE KIND TO THE ENVIRONMENT

THE SIX KINDS OF BEST

KIND TO OTHERS

KIND TO YOURSELF

KIND TO THE ENVIRONMENT

BE

THE LEARNING KIND

THE ACHIEVING KIND

THE COMMUNITY KIND

VALUES EDUCATION PROGRAM

And I am kind to the environment.	American Sign Language for the letter "E."	

CLEAN UP AFTER YOURSELF

- Walk in and around the school buildings to note clean and unclean, and tidy and untidy areas. Discuss what to about improving or maintaining each situation.
- Participate in a weekly or biweekly school competition to see which class or area has the cleanest lunch area, the tidiest bags, etc.
- After recess or lunch, conduct a scavenger hunt to collect litter from the playground. Locate the trash cans which students should have used and discuss possible reasons why students didn't use them. Discuss how playground litter can be reduced.
- Plan and design an imaginative artwork to paint on a school trash can. View designs, select some by voting then make plans to paint the designs on some trash cans near the classroom in groups. (Seek the permission of the principal first!)
- Compose a "rap" or rhyme to encourage others to clean up *or* one which tells how a park, playground, or bedroom feels when it is messy.

KEEP THE LAND, AIR AND WATERWAYS CLEAN

- Collect pictures from magazines of clean and polluted areas to create a class mural.
- Make lists of pollutants under the headings "land," "air" and "water."
- Read the story of "Lester and Clyde" (about two frogs whose pond becomes polluted) and discuss. Paint appropriate pictures about the story.

RECYCLE AND DON'T WASTE

- Cut and sort pictures of various objects according to what they are made of and how they can be reused or recycled.
- Create a recycling collage by asking students to bring pictures of items suitable for recycling. Discuss why we recycle.
- In groups, select three sketches to role-play for other class members to guess. The three sketches should show a recycling, reusing and reducing activity. Students will need to guess what is happening and which category each falls into.

SAVE WATER

- Draw "watery" characters such as a faucet, water drop, or bucket. Attach to a craft stick. Use the characters to talk about ways to save water.
- Students make a "water wise" poster featuring a cartoon character to advise their families about ways in which they can reduce their water consumption.
- In groups, create "musical" pieces using a variety of water words, e.g., "splish," "splash," "plop" and other noises.
- Write a story about an animal family or group of animals who lose their habitat due to drought.

CONSERVE ENERGY

- Complete a crossword puzzle with the clues containing a missing word in a sentence giving hints about conserving energy; e.g., "Turn off unnecessary _____."
- Discuss different forms of transport and the relative amounts of fuel each uses. Students can find and cut out drawings of, for example, aircraft, trucks, cars, motorcycles, bicycles and skateboards to attach to the appropriate labeled sections of a chart. Sections can be labeled "These Use Lots of Fuel," "These Use Some Fuel" and "These Use No Fuel."
- Create a collage or mural using words or headings about gasoline prices, fuel, or different types of energy cut from newspapers. Glue onto brightly colored card stock or paper and cover with a thin layer of watery glue (which dries clear) to form a coating. Display with lists of ways to conserve energy in the classroom and home.

CARE FOR NATURAL HABITATS, WILDLIFE AND ENDANGERED SPECIES

- Complete flow charts of various animals' life cycles to appreciate their individual needs for shelter, food, etc., during their lifetimes.
- Write a story about an endangered animal.
- In small groups or with a partner, design and create a diorama of the habitat of an endangered species.
- Visit a local wildlife area and speak to a ranger or wildlife officer about how best to look after the area for the wildlife that lives there.

USE ENVIRONMENTALLY-FRIENDLY PRODUCTS

- Cut out pictures of environmentally-friendly products from grocery ads to create an informative poster.
- Discuss the problems caused to the environment by plastic bags. Suggest ways for people to carry their groceries home and reduce the need for so many plastic bags.
- Collect a variety of shopping bags. View, discuss and categorize into "environmentally-friendly" and "not environmentally-friendly." Survey to find which are the most widely used by the families of class members.

CONSIDER ENVIRONMENTALLY-FRIENDLY ENERGY SOURCES

- Construct and carry out a survey of common appliances found at home and school, what form of energy each needs to be operated, and if each is environmentally-friendly.
- Survey the students to find out if any of their homes use solar-powered hot water systems. Discuss what they are, why some people buy them, and why they are friendly to the environment.

- On a cold day, try out some "old" ways to keep warm — rub hands together, jump up and down ten times in a row, "Do the Hokey Pokey," etc. Ask students for suggestions for keeping warm without turning on a heater. Repeat and list ways to keep cool on a hot day, such as wetting the face, keeping in the shade, etc.
- Find out what other sources of energy exist (solar, wind, water, etc.), what they are and, as a class, construct a small book to explain how they can be used.

CONSIDER USING RESOURCES THAT CAN BE REPLACED (SUSTAINABLE DEVELOPMENT)

- Place various pieces of "trash" (plastic bags, cloth, paper) and bury them in an area that can't be accessed. Check to see what happens to them after a week, two weeks, a month, etc.
- Make greeting cards using only recycled materials, including cardboard, paper, magazines and cards.
- Plant some vegetables in a large pot or a native tree in the school garden to look after. Discuss why it is a good idea to grow your own food and to plant trees.
- Survey other classmates to discover who has a compost pile at home and how and why they use one. Start one at school!

VALUE OUR CULTURAL HERITAGE

- Learn what the word "artifact" means and identify artifacts on a museum excursion. Students could also bring artifacts or photos of them from home, or speak about them verbally if they can't be brought to school. Examples could be old photos, a trinket box, a fob watch, an antique piece of furniture, etc.
- Students interview older people to find out about customs they value from the past which they want to see continued in the future. Students describe a custom to the class and express a personal opinion about it.
- Visit and sketch various important landmarks. Alternatively, take a digital photo of a landmark and print one for each student to accompany a story or description explaining why it is important to the community.
- Listen to and learn some fun "old" songs to sing at a concert for senior citizens. Examples may include "Mairsie Doates and Doesie Doats," "Don't Sit Under the Apple Tree" and "When You're Smiling."

Introduction

The environment can be defined as the world that exists around us. This is not just the physical conditions of a place, but also includes all those conditions and influences that affect it. Human behavior is responsible for many detrimental changes in the environment and students need to be aware of how they should care for the environment so the things they do have a lessened impact on it.

Worksheet Information

Page 68 – Clean Up After Yourself

- Discuss ways in which students may help to clean up at school and at home.
- If possible show examples of desktop organizers. The students complete the plan as directed on the worksheet and, if desired, make the desktop organizer using their design plan. A range of materials for making the organizers should be provided.

Page 69 – Keep the Land, Air and Waterways Clean

- The student page involves a series of steps to create a mural about pollution using pieces of colored paper torn from magazines.
- Show scenes of polluted rivers, cities, etc. for viewing before commencing the exercise. (NOTE: Sheets of tissue paper may be substituted for paper torn from magazines.)

Page 70 – Recycle and Don't Waste

- What is "recycling"?
- What are some things which can be recycled?
- Students complete the worksheet as directed.

Page 71 – Save Water

- Read and discuss the information.
- Students highlight some important words as they reread the text.
- Create a word search on the board with the students if they have not completed one before. Allow them to try creating their own on the grid provided.

Page 72 – Conserve Energy

- Discuss things in the home and school which are powered by electricity. Demonstrate how to use the code by finishing the first word, then allow students to complete the worksheet as directed.

Page 73 – Care for Natural Habitats, Wildlife and Endangered Species

- Why is it important to care for natural habitats and wildlife?
- How do changes to environments affect the animals and plants that live there?
- Read the definition of a habitat with the students. Discuss the animals and which habitat each may live in. Complete one example with the class, if desired.
- Discuss things which may pollute or change a pond or coral sea environment, and brainstorm suggestions for how these can be avoided or rectified.
- Students may select ideas to complete Question 2.

Page 74 – Use Environmentally-Friendly Products

- What does it mean if something is environmentally-friendly?
- Collect and discuss a variety of different types of environmentally-friendly shopping bags.
- Why are they environmentally-friendly?
- How can you make one of your own which is environmentally-friendly? Encourage students to think "outside the box" for different ideas such as edible shopping bags, etc.
- Allow students to complete the worksheet and share ideas.

Page 75 – Consider Environmentally-Friendly Energy Sources

- The text on page 75 is intended to give students information about an alternative energy source.
- Read the information with the students and allow them to complete the cloze sentences.

Page 76 – Consider Using Resources That Can Be Replaced (Sustainable Development)

- The math activities focus on the use of recycled materials such as empty plastic containers and cardboard boxes. They may be completed in small groups or with a partner. Adult supervision will be required.

Page 77 – Value Our Cultural Heritage

- What interesting things have happened in the past in our local area and how do we know about them?
- Why are some places important to people who live near them?
- How can we look after special places?

Answers

Page 70

2. Some suggestions may include:
   (a) Recycling helps our world!
       Recycling helps our world!
       It reuses junk!
       So have some spunk!
       Recycling helps our world!
   (b) Recycle paper and jars!
       Recycle paper and jars!
       Newspapers can protect your plants!
       Come on and take a stance!
       Recycle paper and jars!

Page 72

1. (a) Turn appliances off when no one is using them.
   (b) Install insulation in homes to reduce energy loss.

Page 73

1.

Arctic	Desert	Grasslands	Tropical Rainforest
polar bear	dingo	elephant	sloth
walrus	rattlesnake	lion	spider monkey
killer whale	camel	jaguar	Ulysses butterfly

Page 75

2. (a) electricity
   (b) pollution
   (c) coal
   (d) electricity
   (e) kites; windmills; sailboats
   (f) wind turbines

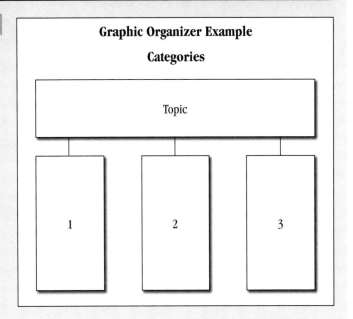

Graphic Organizer Example

Categories

Topic

1   2   3

Desktop Organizer

1. Use the procedure to plan a design for a desktop organizer to help keep your work area clean.

   (a) **Goal**: To design a desktop organizer which is small enough to sit on the desk, easy to use and attractive.

   (b) **Needs**: What will you use to make it? How big will it be? (You may need to measure the space!) What will you use to decorate it?

   (c) **Steps**: Write the steps for making your desktop organizer in the correct order.

   (d) **Test**: How will you know if your design has worked?

   _____

   _____

2. Draw a picture of your design on the back of the worksheet. Be sure to label it clearly.

Murky Mosaic

Pollution is anything which makes the environment dirty.

1. What colors do you think of when you imagine pollution in the air, land, or sea? Orange, pink, gray, or brown? Write a list below.

   _____

   _____

2. Collect some magazines. Tear sections of the colors you listed from pictures in the magazine and group similar colors together.

3. On a large sheet of white paper, carefully sketch a very simple outline of a lake, river, countryside, or city environment using a pencil. Make sure you fill up the whole space.

4. Choose groups of color to place in different sections of the sketch but do not glue them yet.

5. Tear each section of color into small squares and glue onto the places you have chosen. Make sure to overlap the pieces a little.

6. Continue until all sections are covered and you have a mosaic of a murky environment.

7. Write some sentences to describe your picture or some thoughts about completing the activity.

Get the Recycling Rhythm

Recycling is a way to reuse things such as empty bottles, newspapers and old cans. Sometimes they are changed before being made into new things, and sometimes they are used the way they are.

1. Read the rap below.

> Recycle and don't waste!
> Recycle and don't waste!
> Our world is cool!
> Don't be a fool!
> Recycle and don't waste!

2. Use the pattern of the rap above to complete the raps below.

   (a) Recycling helps our world!

   _____

   It reuses junk!

   _____

   _____

   (b) _____

   _____

   Newspapers can protect your plants!

   Come on and take a stance!

   _____

3. With a partner, write some raps on the back of the worksheet using some of the words below.

bottles	cans	waste	junk
mulch	compost	environment	reuse

Water Word Search

1. Read the information about saving water.

Water is a precious resource. We must all try to save water at home and school every day so that we will have enough for the future.

Some easy ways to do this include:

- Turning off faucets while brushing teeth.
- Using timers on sprinklers for the garden.
- Taking short baths or showers.
- Fixing leaking faucets, toilets, or showers.
- Washing cars on the lawn.
- Mulching plants and gardens.
- Watering gardens late in the evening or early in the morning.

2. Use a highlighter to select ten or 12 important words in the text.

3. Starting with the longest words, write words in the grid, making sure to write words through each other going across, down and diagonally. Check each word as you use it.

4. Finally, add a variety of letters to fill up the blank spaces.

Energy Code

We use electricity to cook and keep our food fresh, to wash and dry our clothes, to give light and to make computers, televisions, radios and DVD players work. We need to conserve energy by using electricity carefully.

1. Use the code below to find out two ways to save energy.

A	C	D	E	F	G	H	I	L	M	N	O	P	R	S	T	U	W	Y
1	2	3	4	5	6	7	8	9	10	11	12	13	14	15	16	17	18	19

(a)

16	17	14	11

1	13	13	9	8	1	11	2	4	15

12	5	5

18	7	4	11

11	12

12	11	4

8	15

17	15	8	11	6

16	7	4	10

(b)

8	11	15	16	1	9	9

8	11	15	17	9	1	16	8	12	11

8	11

7	12	10	4	15

16	12

14	4	3	17	2	4

4	11	4	14	6	19

9	12	15	15

2. Use the code and the boxes to write your own message about energy.

72

Natural Habitat

A habitat is the natural place (environment) where an animal or plant lives or grows. Habitats are places such as seas, mountains, or fresh water.

1. Write the animal words under the correct habitat heading.

killer whale	jaguar	sloth	dingo
spider monkey	polar bear	camel	walrus
Ulysses butterfly	lion	elephant	rattlesnake

Arctic	Desert	Grasslands	Tropical Rainforest

2. Write some ideas for caring for the habitats inside each box.

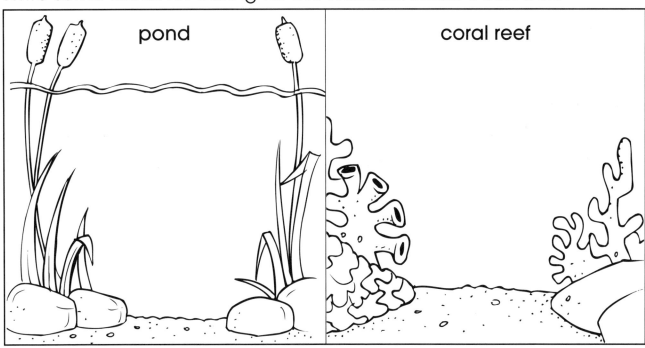

pond

coral reef

My "Kind to the Environment" Bag

1. Write a procedure for creating a shopping bag which is kind to the environment.

(a) Write a title for your procedure.	
(b) What are you going to do?	
(c) List the things you will need.	
(d) Write the steps you will take to make it. Put them in order.	
(e) How will you know if your procedure worked?	

2. Evaluate your environmentally-friendly shopping bag by coloring the appropriate shopping bag below.

| horrible | not very good | not too bad | okay | great | fantastic |

Energy From the Wind

1. Read the information.

> **M**ost homes use electricity from power stations to make their household appliances work. Unfortunately, power stations can cause pollution and use up lots of coal to make electricity.
>
> Have you ever watched a kite flying in the sky? People who fly kites use the power of the wind to move their kites around. The wind also can turn windmills and make sailboats move along the water.
>
> Clever people in different countries around the world are building machines called wind turbines which are moved by the wind and make electricity.

2. Use words from the information to complete the sentences.

   (a) Household appliances are powered by

   _____.

   (b) Power stations cause _____.

   (c) Power stations use _____ to make electricity.

   (d) Coal will not grow again once it is used to make

   _____. It may soon be all gone.

   (e) Wind can be used to make _____ fly in the sky

   and to make _____ and _____ move.

   (f) Machines which use wind power to make electricity are called

   _____.

3. Complete the sentence.

   We need to use wind power more because _____

   _____.

Recycling Math

Choose a math activity about recycled materials to complete.

A. Using protective gloves, collect a pile of garbage. Remove all food and green waste such as garden prunings and grass clippings. Outside or on sheets of newspaper, sort the materials into groups such as cardboard, plastic, metal, glass and other.

Estimate, then weigh each group of garbage and compare the weights.

B. Using protective gloves, collect a variety of empty food containers (cereal boxes, milk cartons, soap boxes, soup cans, etc.). Rinse the cans and milk cartons and shake the boxes to make sure they are as clean as possible.

Measure the length and width of each container and record on a table with the name of each type of container.

C. Select three or four cleaned containers. Record the volume of each container as printed on the side.

Compare two differently-shaped containers which hold the same volume of material.

Discuss why the containers are different.

D. Choose one small and one large container.

Estimate the number of small containers full of material needed to fill the large container.

Use sand or water to compare the estimate with the actual amount of material needed to fill the large container.

E. Using protective gloves, collect a variety of plastic containers.

Sort the containers according to the recycling symbol printed on each container. (There will probably need to be a NO SYMBOLS group.)

Tally and record the results for each group in a table with appropriate symbols at the top of each column.

F. Using protective gloves, collect a variety of recyclable containers.

Select four different types of containers.

In small groups or with a partner, discuss each container and list the physical properties which make it a good choice for holding the material normally in it.

These may include easy to pour, easy to stack, etc.

76

A Special Place

1. Make a list of any places that are important for people in your local area; for example: a museum, an old building, an old gold mine, or a lake.

2. (a) Choose one place and find out more about its history and what makes it special. Write notes.

(b) Design a poster to tell people what is so special about this place, its history, what they can see there and why they should go and see it. Make your poster colorful, eye-catching and informative. Plan your poster, then make it on a large sheet of paper.

78

4. BE THE LEARNING KIND

THE SIX KINDS OF BEST

KIND TO YOURSELF · KIND TO OTHERS · KIND TO THE ENVIRONMENT · KIND TO THE COMMUNITY · THE ACHIEVING KIND · THE LEARNING KIND

BE

VALUES EDUCATION PROGRAM

I am	Have left hand flat, palm upwards, waist height—like a book.	
the learning	Take right hand and sweep the left hand with the back of your hand.	
kind.	Swing your hand up to your head—putting the information from the book into your head.	

BE POSITIVE ABOUT LEARNING

- Help to create a positive atmosphere in the classroom by taking photos of students participating in various learning activities. Students can write a caption or short paragraph to describe what is happening. Display on a pin-up board. Take new photographs at regular intervals and arrange the old photos in a class album.
- Discuss the concept of being "lifelong learners" and that learning does not only happen at school. Make a class list of people who have taught us and what we have learned from each of them. Students can make their own lists.
- Create "snappy" slogans to decorate and display in the room which encourage learning. For example, "We yearn to learn!," "Smart kids keep learning!," "It's cool to be smart!," " We are nerds and proud of it!," etc.

SEEK KNOWLEDGE ABOUT YOURSELF, OTHERS AND THE WORLD AROUND YOU

- Pick an unseen topic from a selection that have been written on slips of paper and placed in a box. Find a book in the classroom or school library to read and learn more about the topic.
- Pose the question, "Is it possible to learn without someone to teach us?" and discuss ways of seeking knowledge and learning about people and the world.
- Provide regular opportunities for students to encounter a wide variety of sources of knowledge. These may include books on a variety of information, access to educational Web sites about animals, history, etc., visits to museums and art galleries, visits from people with interesting skills or occupations, etc.

RECOGNIZE THE VALUE OF KNOWLEDGE

- Solve "What am I?" puzzles with clues about people's occupations.
- Invite students' relatives or people in the community to talk about their jobs and what they have to know to do their job.
- Provide opportunities for students to learn about a particular skill (e.g., china painting, pasta making, kite flying) from an invited guest who can explain how and when he/she learned the skill and how useful it is.
- Use a dictionary to find out what the word "knowledge" means, then write the meaning in your own words. Complete an acrostic using the word "knowledge" and short sentences which tell what it is or involves.

HAVE AN ENQUIRING MIND - BE CURIOUS

- Write a short explanation about how something works; e.g., toy, school item such as a ruler or sharpener, kitchen appliance. Use illustrations or a diagram. Display on a pin-up board or collate into a class book.

- After listening to a story, ask students open-ended "I wonder why . . . ?" and "What would have happened if . . . ?" type questions. Encourage them to formulate some similar questions of their own.
- Write things you want to know on a slip of paper and put it into a box marked with a large question mark. Other students who wish to may select an enquiry, answer it and post the answer in another box marked with a large "A."

DETERMINE HOW YOU LEARN BEST (LEARNING STYLES)

- Find an example of an activity you completed in class that you really enjoyed doing. Explain why you enjoyed it (in written, verbal, or pictorial form, or a combination of the three) to the whole class or small group.
- Explain that some people use different senses to learn and that it can be useful to know if they learn better with their eyes or ears. Set a memory task, e.g., recalling a set of objects. Students compare their recall after listening to the objects being named and after looking at a similar set for one minute.
- Complete a survey to determine favorite learning style(s). For example, a multiple intelligence survey.

HAVE AN OPEN MIND

- Provide story starters from well-known or fictitious origins. Students complete the story and compare endings.
- Rewrite well-known fables or stories from the point of view of the villain or a less-important character.
- Give students simple debate topics such "All students should be allowed to wear whatever they want to school," "Everyone should play sports," etc. Ask students to fold a sheet of paper in half and write reasons "for" on one side and "against" on the other. This activity may be done in small cooperative groups.

BE A CRITICAL THINKER

- View and/or discuss cartoons, children's shows such as *Bob the Builder* and popular children's movies to identify what elements are real or based on real life and what are make believe.
- Students collect advertisements for different brands of a product, e.g., detergent or ice cream, and compare the claims made. Can they all be true? Should you believe everything you read?
- Evaluate and suggest improvements for own stories, artworks, etc.

HAVE A GLOBAL PERSPECTIVE

- Survey the class to find out students' countries of origin and share customs and traditions they may follow or know about.
- Learn traditional songs from other countries. Learn where each country is located and something about its people.
- Hold a regular news week where students must talk about something which has happened in another country. This may be a news item from television or a newspaper clipping, or information about an international sporting event.

SEEK LEARNING OPPORTUNITIES EVERYWHERE

- Discuss computers and what you can learn from them.
- Compile a class list of places where you can go to learn something; e.g., libraries, churches, swimming pools.
- Hold a "learning" session regularly where students share an interesting fact or information learned during the previous week.
- Construct simple books about interesting or unusual topics to add to the class library.

LEARN FROM YOUR MISTAKES

- On a sheet of paper, describe a mistake you have made at school or in your private life. On the back of the sheet, describe what you have done or would do differently.
- Compile a series of sentences which state "When I was five, I used to ... but now I ... " to show how you have learned from your mistakes.

KEEP LEARNING

- Bring an educational board game or card game to school to teach other students who have not played it how to play. Join in with a group to learn a new game yourself.
- Encourage students to contribute to a "Things We Know About ..." board. Contributions to a weekly topic can be written on strips with the child's name and attached to the board and read and discussed each day. The strips can be put into a scrapbook for students to read again later.
- Invite parents to share knowledge about hobbies, skills, or interests they have undertaken so that students will realize that learning does not stop when you are no longer at school.
- Construct a "learning tree" to display on a large board. Each week students write something interesting they have learned onto a leaf shape and add to the tree.

Introduction

Learning enables us to grow as individuals. Learning new things keeps our minds active and makes us more interesting human beings. It is important that children understand the benefits of learning and realize that knowledge gives us more choices and opportunities in our lives. Children and adults should continue to be curious and seek learning opportunities everywhere.

As teachers, we can help children to recognize mistakes as important lessons rather than failures. We can provide learning opportunities in a range of intelligences to enable children to discover the types of learners they are, and we can work towards installing a lifelong love of learning in all our students.

Worksheet Information

Page 84 – Be Positive About Learning

- Sing the first tune with the students. Brainstorm and write simple slogans or sentences about learning on the board to help students write their own lines.
- Students complete Questions 2 and 3 and selected students may volunteer to sing theirs to the class. Note: Students will need to sing words quietly to themselves to see if they fit each tune.

Page 85 – Seek Knowledge About Yourself, Others and the World Around You

- Students may use spare sheets of paper to write answers to their chosen questions.
- Those students who finish quickly may choose other questions to answer.

Page 86 – Recognize the Value of Knowledge

- What jobs do your mom or dad have?
- How did they get these jobs? Why did they get them when other people may have tried to get them as well?
- What do people need before they can get a particular job?
- What is a qualification and how do you get one? A group of parents or other adults will be required.
- Students complete the worksheet as directed. During the interview process, students should become aware that adults need to gain knowledge to do the jobs they want to do.

Page 87 – Have an Enquiring Mind

- Encourage students to imagine what each of the characters would be thinking before trying to write questions to complete the worksheet.

Page 88 – Determine How You Learn Best

- Read and discuss each of the descriptions in (a) before allowing students to check the boxes. This ensures that they understand each fully. Repeat with (b) to (h).
- This checklist based on Multiple Intelligences may indicate that, at this stage, students may have more than one type of learning style.

Page 89 – Have an Open Mind

- Use the activity to foster the idea of keeping an open mind and to consider new ideas. For example, the spider who frightened Miss Muffet might just have been "dropping" in to say hello and didn't mean to frighten her. Discuss what each character did wrong before completing the activity in pairs or individually.
- In the blank box, students can choose their own character from a nursery rhyme, fairy tale, television show, or movie that behaved badly.

Page 90 – Be a Critical Thinker

- Do you believe everything you see and hear?
- Do you have your own opinions about what you see and hear?
- What is real and what is make-believe on the TV?

Page 91 – Have a Global Perspective

- Were you or any of your relatives born in another country?
- Do you or any of your relatives speak another language?
- Have you visited another country?
- What have you learned about other countries from watching television?

Page 92 – Seek Learning Opportunities Everywhere

- What are some things you have learned at different stages of your life?
- Who helped you or where did you learn these things?
- Who or where are people or places to help you to learn?

Page 93 – Learn From Your Mistakes

- What is a mistake you have made? What did you learn from it?
- How can mistakes help you to learn and grow?

Page 94 – Keep Learning

- Do you only learn at school? Where else do you learn?
- Why is it important to keep learning all through your life?

Answers

Page 84

2. One suggestion is:

Learning can be so much fun!

It is good for everyone!

Read some books and listen well!

'Til you hear the home time bell!

Learning can be so much fun!

It is good for everyone!

Page 90

• Ladybugs are insects. They are a kind of beetle. They have a small, round body. Ladybugs have wings and six legs. They can walk (delete "sing") and fly. Ladybugs have two antennae on their head. Their antennae help them to find things. Most ladybugs are brightly colored/black with red spots. Ladybugs can be found on plants. They eat insects that are pests.

Page 91

1. Hindi – namaste; Italian – ciao; French – âllo; Japanese – konnichiwa; Welsh – hwyl

2. Hindi – alavidha; Italian – ciao; French – au revoir; Japanese – sayonara; Welsh – da bo chi

Graphic Organizer Example

Concept Charts

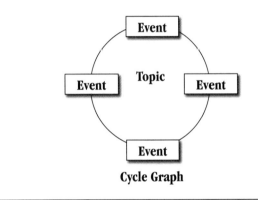

Know–Wonder–Learned Chart

Cycle Graph

Learning Songs

1. Sing the following song to the tune "*Frere Jacques.*"

I love learning.
I love learning.
So should you!
So should you!
Learning makes me smarter!
Learning makes me smarter!
And you too!
And you too!

2. Complete the words to match the tune "*Twinkle, Twinkle, Little Star.*"

Learning can be so much fun!
It is good for everyone!

_____

_____

Learning can be so much fun!
It is good for everyone!

3. Write another song to encourage others to learn using the tune
"*Itsy Bitsy Spider.*"

84

Learning Questions

1. Select one question from each column and decide how to find the answer.

Yourself	Others	The World
(a) Where was your father's mother (your grandmother) born and in what year?	(a) Which class member has his/her birthday the closest to yours?	(a) What is the smallest country in the world?
(b) Choose one of your talents and find out who you might have inherited it from.	(b) Which class members have a family almost the same as yours?	(b) What language is the most commonly spoken around the world and how many countries is it spoken in?
(c) What does your surname mean and where did it come from?	(c) Who are your brother or sister's favorite singers?	(c) What food is eaten the most around the world?
(d) What would four generations of your family tree look like?	(d) What is the name of the place where your mom and dad work and what do they do there?	(d) Which country in the world has the most people?

2. Record your answers on a sheet of paper to include in a loose-leaf "answers" book to be kept in the room for others to read. Be sure to staple a copy of the question to your answer and write your name on the back.

3. Write a question of your own for others to answer.

Occupations Interview

Adults usually have to learn special skills or information to be able to do their job. Many must have training at a special school, university, or college or learn skills "on the job."

Complete the interview questions for a parent or adult you know well.

What is your full name?	
What is your occupation?	
Where do you work?	
How long have you been doing your current job?	
What qualifications or training do you have?	
What work experience have you had?	
What do you like about your job?	
What do you dislike about your job?	
Do you have any other qualifications?	

86

Be a Curious Cat

1. Write one question to ask the following characters.

(a) *Cinderella*

_____

_____

(b) *The bear who went over the mountain*

_____

_____

(c) *The mouse who ran up the clock*

_____

_____

(d) *The ugly duckling*

_____

_____

(e) *Itsy Bitsy Spider*

_____

_____

(f) *Jack or Jill*

_____

_____

(g) *One of the King's men who couldn't put Humpty Dumpty back together again*

_____

_____

How Do You Learn Best?

1. Check the words below which best describe you.

(a) *Word-wise learners can be:*

word wizards.............. ☐   story scribblers ....☐   super spellers ....☐
private poets................☐   ravenous readers ....☐   news narrators..............☐

(b) *Body-wise learners can be:*

sporty samplers ....☐   drama dabblers............☐   "feely" fellows...............☐
wriggly worms..............☐   crafty creatures............☐   daffy "doers" ....☐

(c) *Logic-wise learners can be:*

curious kids..................☐   game guzzlers ....☐   scary scientists ....☐
puzzle players ....☐   problem solvers...........☐   number nuts.................☐

(d) *Picture-wise learners can be:*

avid artists ....☐   jigsaw jigglers ....☐   dapper drawers ....☐
map readers.................☐   model makers ....☐   dynamic dreamers ....☐

(e) *Nature-wise learners can be:*

nutty naturalists ....☐   animal carers..............☐   great gardeners ....☐
outdoors ogres.............☐   zoo zombies ....☐   environment experts ......☐

(f) *Music-wise learners can be:*

super singers ....☐   manic musicians..........☐   tempo tappers ....☐
music listeners..............☐   rote singers ....☐   rap rhymers ....☐

(g) *People-wise learners can be:*

team players ....☐   group workers ....☐   idea sharers ....☐
friendly fellows..............☐   people persons ....☐   happy for others ....☐

(h) *Self-wise learners can be:*

solo workers................☐   thinkers about future ....☐   thinkers about feelings...☐
homebodies ....☐   have few close friends ..☐   diary writers ....☐

2. Count the number of checks for each section and complete the sentence.

I am mostly a _____ learner.

I'm Not Really Bad

The characters below have all behaved badly in a nursery rhyme or fairy tale. But were they really bad?

1. (a) Imagine you are each character. In each speech bubble, explain that you weren't really being bad and what you were really trying to do.

   (b) In the blank box, draw and write about a character of your own choice.

The spider who frightened Miss Muffet	The troll in *"The Three Billy Goats Gruff"*
Goldilocks	

Ladybugs

The report about ladybugs below has many incorrect facts. Use your own knowledge and the school library to rewrite the report so it is correct.

Ladybugs are mammals. They are a kind of beetle. .... (1 error)
They have a large, round body. Ladybugs have wings and eight legs.
They can walk, sing, and fly. .... (3 errors)
Ladybugs have three antennae on their head.
Their antennae help them to walk. .... (2 errors)
Most ladybugs are yellow. Ladybugs can be found in the ocean.
They eat fish that are pests. .... (3 errors)

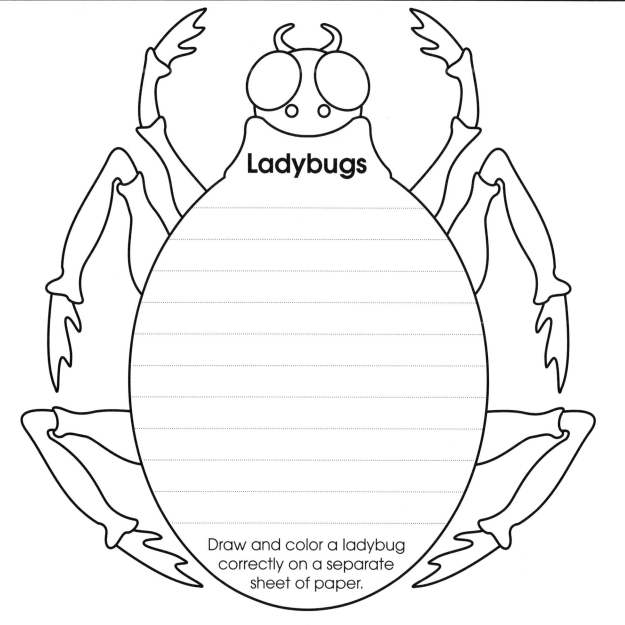

Ladybugs

Draw and color a ladybug correctly on a separate sheet of paper.

90

Hello! Goodbye!

Did you know there are about 3,000 different languages in the world?

1. Follow the maze to find out how to say "hello" in each language.

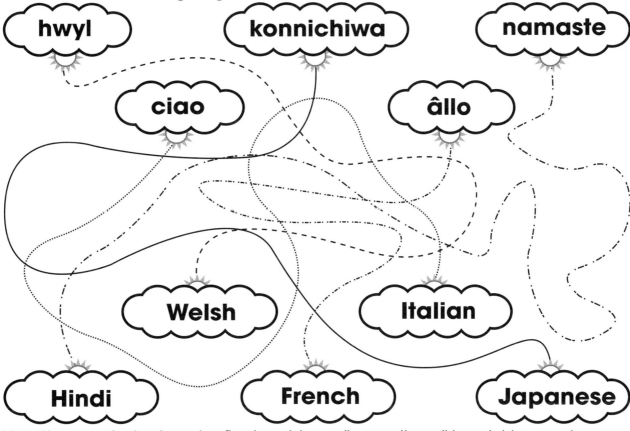

2. Use the code below to find out how "goodbye" is said in each language.

a	b	c	d	e	f	g	h	i	j	k	l	m	n	o	p	q	r	s	t	u	v	w	x	y	z
❀	❁	✳	❄	❅	❆	✴	✺	✻	✼	✶	●	○	■	❑	❐	❒	❏	▲	▼	◆	❖	◗	❘	❙	❚

Hindi   (❀●❀❖❄❄✳✴❀)   _____

Italian   (✳❄❀❑)   _____

Japanese (✳❑■■❄❄❄❄◗❀)   _____

Welsh   (❄❀ ○❑ ❄❄❄)   _____

French   (❀◆ ❑❄❖❑✳❑)   _____

Library Plan

Design a school library using some or all of the items below. You can also draw other features you think should go in a library.

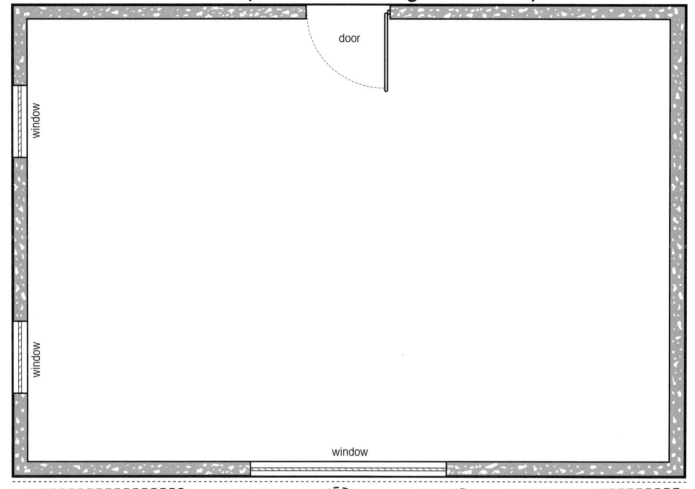

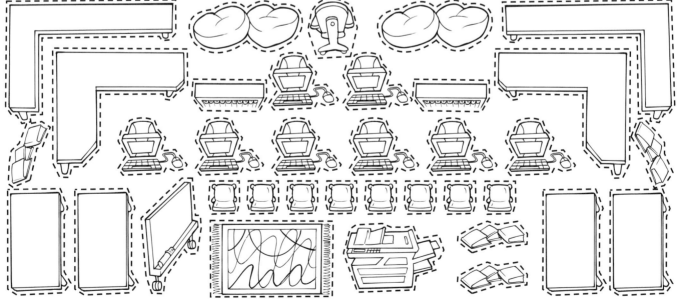

© World Teachers Press® • www.worldteacherspress.com

The Hare and the Tortoise

1. Read the fable.

Once upon a time there was a tortoise and a hare. The tortoise was a quiet, friendly fellow who did things slowly. The hare was a show and he was always in a hurry, running everywhere. He liked to make fun of everyone, especially the tortoise because he was so slow.

The tortoise became tired of the hare teasing him and decided to do something about it.

"I may be slow, but I can beat you in a race."

The hare laughed. "We will have a race tomorrow across the fields, through the woods until we reach the creek, and back again."

The next day all the animals came to watch the race. The hare raced off quickly, while the tortoise plodded along slowly. When the hare reached the creek, he decided to stop for a rest. The tortoise was such a long way behind and the hare knew he couldn't catch up. He sat down and leaned against a tree. It was warm in the sun, and soon the hare fell asleep.

Later on, the tortoise reached the creek and saw the sleeping hare. He continued slowly and steadily back towards the finishing line. All the animals began to cheer loudly, which woke the hare. He ran back as fast as he could, but the tortoise crossed the line first. The hare could not believe it.

"See," said the tortoise, "I said I could beat you! It is better to be slow and steady and win the race."

2. Answer the questions.

   (a) If the hare was so fast, why did the tortoise win the race?

   _____

   _____

   (b) What do you think the hare could learn from his mistake?

   _____

   _____

New Games, Old Games

From the moment we were born to the day we will die, we should all continue to learn new things. One way of doing this is to talk to a grandparent or elderly friend or relative. You will find out how much they know about the past and how they are still learning new things.

An interesting topic to talk to them about is what kind of games they played when they were your age. Ask an elderly person you know the following questions.

Name _____   Age _____

What was your favorite game when you were about my age?

_____

How did you play it? _____

_____

_____

What games did you play outdoors?	What games did you play indoors?
_____	_____
_____	_____
_____	_____

What games, toys, or sporting equipment did you have?

_____

_____

What do you think has changed the most about games played now compared to the past?

_____

_____

5. BE THE ACHIEVING KIND

THE SIX KINDS OF BEST

KIND TO OTHERS
KIND TO THE ENVIRONMENT
KIND THE COMMUNITY
KIND THE ACHIEVING
KIND THE LEARNING
KIND TO YOURSELF
BE

VALUES EDUCATION PROGRAM

I am the achieving kind.	Point upwards—aim for the stars.	

GIVE IT A TRY!

- Award merit certificates or merit badges or distribute stickers to those students who "give it a try" and don't fear failure.
- Allow students to give short talks to tell about something new they have tried. Ask them to find one positive thing to say about having attempted the activity, whether it was successful or not.
- Create rap-like movements to sayings such as "Don't get yourself in a stew, try something new."

TRY LOTS OF DIFFERENT THINGS

- During "activity" or "freeplay" time, set out and constantly change activities on a regular basis so that at least one activity is completely new and uses different skills or processes.
- Convert a well-known poem or rhyme to a mime, musical piece, drama, or mathematical code.
- Survey the class to graph activities students have tried or do after school or on weekends to see if others might like to try them.

DISCOVER WHAT YOU'RE GOOD AT AND ENJOY DOING

- Students sit in a circle and one after another state one thing that they think they are good at. The other students raise their hand if they agree. Those with hands down may be called upon to state something else they think the chosen student is good at.
- Fold a sheet of paper into two. On one side write "Things I Am Good At" and on the other side write "Things I Enjoy." Complete both columns and compare the items on each list. Discuss.
- Students write a description of what they are good at and enjoy doing and draw an appropriate illustration. Compile into a class booklet or display for others to read.

DO THINGS TO THE BEST OF YOUR ABILITY

- Place gold stars or stickers upon all work that is completed well. Students may give suggestions for any ways to improve their own work.
- Complete two identical pictures by coloring. The first should be done unaided with no time restrictions or guidance. The second should be done slowly with teacher guidance as to colors for different sections, etc.
- Students view samples of their written work and art and craft work and decide which have been completed to the best of their ability and which can be improved.

PURSUE QUALITY AND PERSONAL EXCELLENCE

- Encourage self-evaluation by asking the students to say, "I think my work is … but I think it will be even better next time if I … ."
- Create merit certificates for achieving excellence or improving in an area such as neatness, spelling, or cooperation.

USE YOUR TALENTS

- Hold a special afternoon where students are able to relate or show something they are good at to others. This may include sporting activities, singing, musical talents, etc.
- Hold a talent show to raise money for a specific charity such as the Red Cross or Habitat for Humanity.
- Students use their talents to teach a classmate, younger student, sibling, etc., how to do or improve something; e.g., a dance, how to play chess, using shading more effectively on a coloring activity.

DEVELOP A SENSE OF PURPOSE

- Discuss occupations and ask students to select one they would like to do. Identify the nature of the occupation and what skills, talents and training they would need. Students draw a picture of themselves in the future doing this job.
- Wear a blindfold and try to guess an object by touch, with the only clues allowed explaining the purpose or use of the object.
- Match equipment and uniforms to the correct occupations and explain the purpose of each item.
- Write or draw things which are important to you. Display these on a banner, an honor board, or decorative certificate.

MANAGE YOUR TIME EFFECTIVELY

- Play "Beat the clock." Record how long it takes to do daily tasks; e.g., packing away equipment or lining up. Try to improve on the previous time taken, so that you don't "waste time."
- Begin a simple diary which includes when homework is due, things to remember to bring to school such as library books and items for "News," leisure-time activities and important events such as family birthdays and special school days.
- Reward students with verbal praise or with a sticker or merit certificate for being punctual after break time and not wasting time in class with unnecessary talking, etc.

MANAGE YOUR MONEY WISELY

- Discuss saving money to buy a special item. Students then make a papier mâché money box in an animal shape.
- Complete money problems which give practice using money to buy objects with a set amount of money.
- Devise strategies for using pocket money for saving up for a specific gift for another person or budgeting for a toy, magazine, CD, or game for yourself.
- Stimulate interest in managing money by comparing coins and coin names from other countries.

SET WORTHWHILE GOALS AND MAKE PLANS TO ACHIEVE THEM

- Set a daily class goal and discuss what students need to do to achieve this goal. The goal should be displayed and success evaluated at the end of the day.
- Construct a "goal tower" out of recycled cartons or containers. Add an item to the tower every time a class or individual goal is achieved.

SHOW PERSISTENCE AND SELF-DISCIPLINE TO ACHIEVE GOALS

- Complete activities such as coloring intricate tessellation designs or completing a series of spelling or mathematical problems. These may be done to indicate that persistence allows us to reach our goals. (In this case, completing a series of activities or an intricate design.)
- Practice skills relating to events in an upcoming sports carnival.
- Discuss if students have any uncompleted tasks at home; e.g., an unfinished book, jigsaw puzzle, Lego™ construction. How should they persist to finish the task? Also relate to incomplete or missed chores such as walking the dog or tidying their room.

LOOK AT DIFFERENT WAYS OF DOING THINGS – CREATIVITY AND INNOVATION

- Students listen to fables and give suggestions for different ways the animals may solve the problems.
- Different groups discuss how to solve the same problem and role-play how they would solve it. Discuss different groups' solutions.
- Create dance movements or lyrics to accompany a specific piece of music. This activity may be done individually, in pairs, or in groups.
- Identify variations in the way people do the same things; e.g., how they fold clothes or make spaghetti and meatballs. Discuss how there is often more than one way of doing something successfully.

DEVELOP GOOD COMMUNICATION SKILLS

- Play "Telephone" to demonstrate the importance of speaking clearly and listening to and remembering what is said.
- Find the definition of "communication." Discuss the different forms of communication used in the classroom and list ways to improve them.
- Create a mural of methods of communicating such as telephone, e-mail, television, radio, SMS message, fax, etc. Use individual sketches or pictures cut from magazines, catalogs, or newspapers.
- Students plan a news-telling item, science talk, etc., using a "Who? What? When? Where? Why?" format. Others listen and fill out a sheet with the same questions to find out if they listened carefully.

SEEK GOOD ROLE MODELS

- Discuss the type of person the students admire and would wish to be like. Talk about reasons these people are admired; e.g., their appearance, achievements, success, kindness, personality. Create a collage of pictures of students' selected role models.
- Select a specific sporting or media personality or world figure to research. Record information for a simple oral or written presentation. Include information which tells why he/she is a good role model.
- Read or listen to narrative stories and decide whether the characters are good or bad role models.

Introduction

To discover what it is we are good at and enjoy doing, it is necessary to try out a range of different experiences and activities—especially when we are children. Students need to understand that they will have to take risks and overcome feelings such as fear to achieve something worthwhile in life. Other qualities or skills, such as persistence and time management, are also important, and are worth exploring and learning about.

Worksheet Information

Page 100 – Give It a Try!

- Enlarge and use the awards to present to students who attempt new things (whether they succeed or not). Students may decorate the awards themselves.

Page 101 – Try Lots of Different Things

- Discuss a variety of new things which students may have tried. Compare the opinions of other students who may have tried the same activity and discuss the differences.
- Students may complete the worksheet as directed.

Page 102 – Discover What You're Good At and Enjoy Doing

- Students color the appropriate number of stars to indicate how good they think they are at doing each activity. (One star for an activity which they think they are not very good at and five for an activity which they think they are very good at!)
- Students check those activities which they enjoy doing whether they are good at them or not.

Page 103 – Do Things to the Best of Your Ability

- Glue or photocopy the enlarged frame onto card stock. Allow the students to decorate it and use it to display a piece of their best work each week.

Page 104 – Pursue Quality and Personal Excellence

- Two completed activities are given for students to examine and improve. Spaces are provided for students to complete each activity again in a better fashion than the one given.

Page 105 – Use Your Talents

- Students need to identify what they are good at first before knowing how to use their talents. Often other people can see talents which we may not notice in ourselves.
- Students complete the worksheet as directed.

Page 106 – Develop a Sense of Purpose

- Students need to find out what is important to them. These things give purpose to the things they do now and in the future. Some aspects may lead to later decisions about careers.
- Students analyze the symbol which tells about Jake, then list things which are important to them before using them to create their own symbol. Students may include parts of items chosen to include in their symbol.

Page 107 – Manage Your Time Effectively

- Students write a general list of things which they would normally do. These should include going to school, sports training, watching television, playing on the computer, etc.
- Students then complete Questions 2 and 3 as directed.
- For Question 4, students may suggest ways to find more time to fit in other activities, such as doing homework by reducing the amount of time watching television or playing on the computer.
- For Question 5, students should suggest words such as "saver" to complete the sentence.

Page 108 – Manage Your Money Wisely

- Although the students are completing a variety of sums about money, the activities aim to make them aware that by using their money wisely (saving a little regularly), they will be able to save enough to pay for a special purchase.

Page 109 – Set Worthwhile Goals and Make Plans to Achieve Them

- What is a goal? Read the definition at the bottom of the worksheet with the students. What are short-term goals and long-term goals? Give examples.
- Students may discuss with a partner some answers for each type of goal for Question 1, then complete the worksheet.

Page 110 – Show Persistence and Self-Discipline to Achieve Your Goals

- Students complete the worksheet as directed. Note: This fable may also be used to introduce a discussion about different ways of doing things (page 113).

Page 111 – Look at Different Ways of Doing Things – Creativity and Innovation

- Students are given three different tasks to achieve the same aim, which is to encourage others to "be the achieving kind." This activity aims to show students that there are different ways to do the same thing.

Page 112 – Develop Good Communication Skills

- Discuss what is happening in each picture, then allow students to write an appropriate response for the child in the picture to say.

Page 113 – Seek Good Role Models

- Students complete the worksheet as directed. Selected students may read their work to relate the type of qualities which are desirable in a role model.

Answers

Page 108

1. (a) $24
   (b) $5
   (c) $13
   (d) $10

Page 110

2. "Persistence" is the action or fact of persisting; the quality of being persistent; continued existence or occurrence.

4. "Self-discipline" – discipline and training of oneself, usually for improvement.

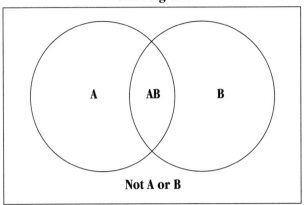

Graphic Organizer Example

Venn Diagrams

A   AB   B

Not A or B

Cartoon and Picture Strips

Picture 1	Picture 2	Picture 3	Picture 4	Picture 5

"Give It a Try" Awards

Presented to

....

for "giving it a try"

signed ....

date ....

Presented to

....

for "giving it a try"

signed ....

date ....

PRESENTED TO

....

FOR "GIVING IT A TRY"

signed ....

date ....

Presented to

....

for "giving it a try"

signed ....

date ....

PRESENTED TO

....

FOR "GIVING IT A TRY"

signed ....

date ....

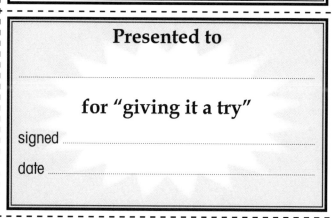

Presented to

....

for "giving it a try"

signed ....

date ....

PRESENTED TO

....

FOR "GIVING IT A TRY"

signed ....

date ....

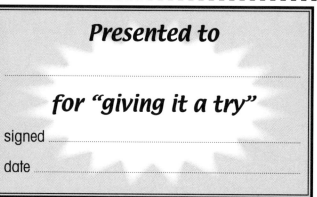

Presented to

....

for "giving it a try"

signed ....

date ....

Different Things

1. Complete the shapes.

(a) Write five new foods or meals you have tried in the last few months.

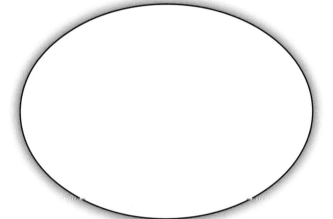

(b) Write the names of five new people you have talked to in the last few months.

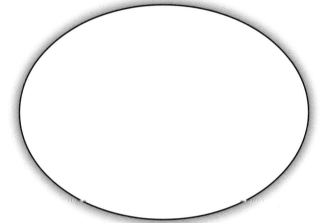

(c) Write the names of five new books you have read in the last few months.

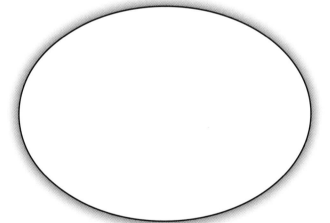

(d) Write the names of five new things you have tried in the last few months.

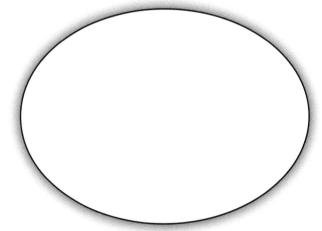

2. Write or draw one new thing to try in the next few months in each column of the table.

One New Fruit or Vegetable	One New Hobby or Leisure Activity

101

How Good Are You?

1. Color the stars to show how good you are at doing each thing.

Home						
making your bed	☆	☆	☆	☆	☆	
cleaning your room	☆	☆	☆	☆	☆	
helping with chores	☆	☆	☆	☆	☆	
getting ready for school	☆	☆	☆	☆	☆	
keeping myself healthy	☆	☆	☆	☆	☆	
School						
reading a book	☆	☆	☆	☆	☆	
writing a story	☆	☆	☆	☆	☆	
solving math problems	☆	☆	☆	☆	☆	
drawing a picture	☆	☆	☆	☆	☆	
finding out how things work	☆	☆	☆	☆	☆	
working with others	☆	☆	☆	☆	☆	
helping the teacher	☆	☆	☆	☆	☆	
Other						
playing a sport	☆	☆	☆	☆	☆	
helping other people	☆	☆	☆	☆	☆	
talking in front of others	☆	☆	☆	☆	☆	
role-playing or acting	☆	☆	☆	☆	☆	
trying new things	☆	☆	☆	☆	☆	

2. Put a check in the box at the end of each row if you enjoy doing that thing (even if you're not good at it!).

© World Teachers Press® • www.worldteacherspress.com

My Best Work

Color and paint the frame carefully, and use it to display a piece of your best work each week.

Excellent Job!

1. Complete the activities again but make each better than that given.

(a) Writing a story

Once a dog lost her way home. She followed her nose and went up and down the streets until she found her way back home.

_____

_____

_____

_____

_____

_____

_____

(b) Drawing a picture

Talents Interview

Most people have one or more talents for doing something special. Others are able to work hard to learn special skills and abilities.

1. Survey four class members to find out what **they** think **your** talents are.

    (a) Student 1 _____

    (b) Student 2 _____

    (c) Student 3 _____

    (d) Student 4 _____

2. Complete the sentences.

    (a) I think I have a talent for _____

    _____

    _____ .

    (b) I could use my talent to _____

    _____

    _____ .

3. Complete the sentence.

    (a) I would like to have a talent for _____

    _____

    _____ .

    (b) I could develop this talent by _____

    _____

    _____ .

Important Things

1. The symbol below tells us about Jake. Write the things which you think are important to him.

Jake's Symbol

_____

_____

_____

_____

_____

2. Make a list of **ten** things which are important to you. You might include people (such as friends and family members), pets, things you like to do, special places, or special things (such as a favorite toy, book, or belonging given to you by a grandparent).

_____   _____

_____   _____

_____   _____

_____   _____

_____   _____

3. Choose **five** of the things listed above and use them to draw a symbol which tells about you and the things that are important to you.

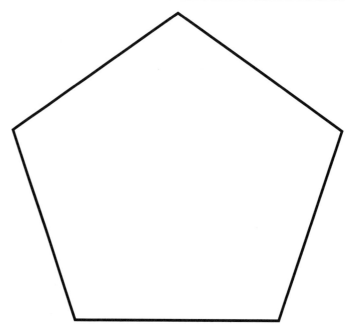

Don't Be a Time Waster!

1. On the clock face, write lots of different things which you would do in one day. Two have been done for you.

2. List activities which you **don't spend enough** time doing.

_____

_____

_____

_____

_____

3. List activities which you spend **too much** time doing.

_____

_____

_____

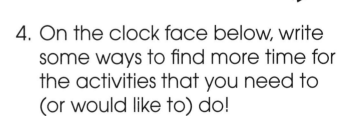

4. On the clock face below, write some ways to find more time for the activities that you need to (or would like to) do!

5. Complete the sentence.

I'm not a time waster, I'm a time

_____.

Money Sums

1. Solve the money problems. Show how you worked them out.

   (a) Gillian saved $2.00 each week from her allowance. How much money did she save in 12 weeks?

   (c) Maria saved $5.00 towards her mom's birthday present and her brother Angelo saved $8.00. How much did they save altogether?

   (b) Robbie saved $20.00 over four weeks. How much did he have to save each week?

   (d) Dad gave both Daniel and Alex $5.00 for doing extra chores. They wanted to buy a toy together for $20.00. How much more money do they need?

2. Work out how much money you could save for something special (such as a present for someone you love or a special toy) if you save some of your allowance for 12 weeks or more.

108

Setting Goals

1. Choose one goal for each section and write the steps you will need to take to achieve each.

Goal:

Goal:

Goal:

(a) Goals Which Take a Short Time

(b) Goals Which Take a Bit Longer

(c) Goals Which Take a Long Time

2. Write and draw about your most successful goal.

_____

_____

_____

Goal: Something which needs effort to achieve; a purpose or end.

The Crow and the Pitcher

1. Read the fable about a persistent crow.

> *Once a very thirsty crow found a pitcher which still had some water in it. The pitcher had a long neck, and the crow could not reach the water. The crow thought he would soon die of thirst. He tried and tried but he could not reach the water.*
>
> *Finally, he thought of a plan. He collected lots of small pebbles. One by one, he dropped them into the pitcher. Each time he dropped a pebble into the water, the water level rose higher and higher. Soon the level of the water reached the top of the pitcher, and the clever crow was able to drink enough water to save his own life.*

2. Write the meaning of the word "persistence" from the dictionary.

_____

_____

3. Rewrite the meaning in your own words.

_____

_____

4. Find and write the meaning of "self-discipline."

_____

_____

5. List some things which you have achieved through persistence and self-discipline.

- _____

- _____

- _____

- _____

Which Way?

Complete the three different activities in the spaces provided.

1. Design and draw a poster encouraging others to "Be the achieving kind."

2. Write a slogan or catchy jingle to encourage others to "Be the achieving kind."

3. Write a short story in which one character encourages the other to "Be the achieving kind."

Communication Cartoons

Complete the speech bubbles to show what should be said in each situation.

Good Role Models

1. Read the rhyme.

I look at you and what do I see?
An interesting person I'd like to be!
You are so great because you do
All the things I'd like to do too!

You don't give up! You do your best!
You're so much better than all the rest!
So I hope you don't mind if I choose you
To be my role model. I'll do as you do!

2. Select four adults who would be good role models. Draw them, label the pictures and write a sentence to tell why each would be a good role model.

6. BE THE COMMUNITY KIND

| I am the community kind. | Form an "A" shape in front of your body with your fingers—like a house. |  |

BE THE COMMUNITY KIND – OVERVIEW

BEHAVE RESPONSIBLY

- After a discussion about looking after themselves and their belongings, students can draw a picture of themselves doing this at home. An individual caption could be added; e.g., " I look after my . . ."
- Role-play the correct and incorrect way to behave in a certain situation; e.g., leaving an apple core on the ground in the lunch area instead of putting it in the trash can.
- Make a list of bad habits which annoy, irritate and disturb others. Devise ways to deal with these sensitively so that responsible behavior is displayed.
- Write a song titled "Bad Habits."
- List the responsibilities you have at home and school and write a short job description for each.

RESPECT AUTHORITY

- Draw a school "tree" which shows the principal at the top and other relevant staff members on the branches. Talk about what responsibilities each has at school.
- Organize class visits from people in occupations of authority such as the police or fire department, or excursions to their place of work. Plan questions to ask before the visit.
- Learn songs or percussion pieces about people in authority such as ambulance drivers and police officers.
- Brainstorm to list jobs in authority and identify what these people are in charge of. Examples could include coach, umpire, police officer, principal, or parent.

FOLLOW RULES

- Students determine a set of appropriate rules for different class activities; e.g., playing in the home corner, using sports equipment. Consider safety and equity issues.
- Write an imaginative story or poem about a city or town which has no rules.
- View scenes of children not following rules at school, the swimming pool, the beach, playground, etc. Identify how they should be behaving.

BE HONEST AND SEEK TRUTH

- Read the story of Pinocchio, the boy whose nose grew longer every time he lied. Play "Pin the Nose on Pinocchio"!
- Discuss specific scenarios such as not telling mom or dad the truth if you accidentally break a vase or window. Why do people lie? What are the consequences?
- Complete the sentence "An honest person ..." to tell about things which honest people do and say.
- Create a double-sided puppet on a large craftstick. One side has the face or outline of an honest person and the other has that of a dishonest person. Discuss how appearances can be deceptive.

- Write an acrostic poem using the letters in words such as "honesty" or "truth."

SHOW INTEGRITY – DEVELOP A SENSE OF WHAT'S MORALLY AND ETHICALLY RIGHT, AND ACT THAT WAY

- Students make good choices from two ways to act in given situations, such as finding a wallet on the sidewalk, etc.
- Listen to the song "Give a Little Whistle" from the Walt Disney version of *Pinocchio,* where Jiminy Cricket sings about "letting your conscience be your guide." Talk about the lyrics and what they mean.
- Read and discuss the story of "The Boy Who Cried Wolf." Discuss how the boy did not show integrity nor act morally and the consequences that occurred.

BE USEFUL

- Discuss how you feel after you have done something really useful and helped someone. Make a list of useful things you can do at home and school and who you would help.
- Identify people in the community who volunteer to help at your school (e.g., cafeteria or snack bar workers, parent helpers in the classroom) as well as those in the wider community, such as Meals on Wheels drivers, charity fund-raisers and caregivers in retirement homes.
- Compose a poem about being useful. Use a format such as acrostic, haiku, string, or shape poem.

GET INVOLVED IN THE COMMUNITY

- As a class, create a large map of the local community to display in the classroom or library. Label with the facilities available.
- Complete an eight-page booklet about things the students like to do in their community; e.g., play at the local park, go to the library.
- Invite a Girl Scout, Brownie or Boy Scout leader or rotary member to talk to the class about their organizations and how the students or their parents may become members.

STRIVE FOR JUSTICE AND A FAIR CHANCE FOR ALL

- Students take turns to talk about their homes, customs, family, traditions, etc. (to develop awareness of valuing diversity).
- Learn how to say hello in different languages.
- Have parents assist students in preparing food from different countries to taste and compare.
- Read or write a story about a child from another country who is ostracized because he/she looks different.
- Discuss the importance of fair play in all kinds of games and sports; e.g., card games, hide and seek, baseball and marbles.

SHARE WITH AND CARE FOR THOSE IN NEED

- Visit a local senior citizens home or aged care home to talk, play games with and perform plays or other concert items for its residents. Visit once each term.
- Invite a parent to bring a baby into the class and discuss how dependent babies are and the kind of care they need. Encourage students to ask questions and to relate ways in which they could help a baby.
- Students participate in raising or donating funds for a nominated worthy cause they are able to relate to.
- Find other words which rhyme with "share" and "care." Write a poem using the words.

SUPPORT RECONCILIATION

- Fold a long sheet of paper accordian-style (use wide sections). Draw an outline of a child on the front. Cut around the outline on the folded side. Open out to form a "chain" of children holding hands. Draw and color the outlines to make children of different nationalities.
- Create a "Colorful World" mural using pictures of children from all countries around the world cut from magazines and glued onto colored card stock.

CONTRIBUTE TO RESEARCH

- Encourage students to donate a coin to make a money chain for medical research.
- Learn about charities which help to fund research into illnesses in children.
- Create a colorful poster to advertise a fund-raising activity at school.
- Save up allowance to make a donation to a medical charity.

SUPPORT FREEDOM

- Discuss the things children would not be able to do if they lived in a country at war.
- Write simple arguments "for" and "against" the topic "People should be able to say what they think." Discuss your results.

STRIVE FOR PEACE

- Discuss and generate a list of what students think of when they hear the word "peace."
- Listen to some songs from the 1960s which talk about peace. Find some modern songs which have the same message.
- Make up a peace hand sign of your own.

Introduction

The community refers to any group of people, ranging from close family and friends in the local neighborhood to the population of all countries around the world. By being the community kind, we are playing our part to strive for a peaceful, harmonious life for all. This requires compromise and understanding from individuals and a willingness to follow order for the good of the community.

Worksheet Information

Page 120 – Behave Responsibly
- What does it mean to behave responsibly? Discuss.
- Students complete the worksheet as directed.

Page 121 – Respect Authority
- Read and explain the definition of "authority."
- Students complete Question 1 as directed.
- Read and explain the definition of "respect," then allow students to complete Question 2.

Page 122 – Follow Rules
- What rules do you have at home to follow?
- What rules do we have at school to follow?
- Why do we have these rules? Discuss.
- Read the comments on the board game with the students and discuss how the game might be played.
- Students complete Question 2 independently.

Page 123 – Be Honest and Seek Truth
- What does it mean to be honest? Discuss.
- Students complete the worksheet as directed.

Page 124 – Show Integrity
- What does "integrity" mean? What does it mean to have or show integrity?
- How do you know what is the right thing to do and how to act?
- Read and discuss each scenario as a class, with a partner, or in small groups. Discuss possible solutions to each scenario.

Page 125 – Be Useful
- While students are completing this exercise, they should be thinking about different ways to be useful in each area. They will also realize that by being useful, they will feel good about themselves.
- Students complete the worksheet as directed.

Page 126 – Get Involved in the Community
- Brainstorm and list community activities which students may have attended such as agricultural shows, clean-up days, fairs, etc.
- If possible, show advertisements from magazines of musical events and displays or open days for students to view.
- Allow students to complete the worksheet as directed.

Page 127 – Strive for Justice and a Fair Chance for All
- Students should be aiming to be "fair" people.
- Read and discuss the information with the students. Divide the students into small groups to discuss the information.
- Students may now complete the worksheet as directed.

Page 128 – Share With and Care For Those in Need
- Brainstorm a list of people who may be in need. This may include people the students know and people who have suffered a disaster in another country.
- Discuss the pictures and ways to help the people in the pictures. Suggestions may include: (a) saying nice things to help the boy with the sick cat feel better or keeping him company while he watches his pet; (b) sharing a portion of lunch; (c) reading to the lonely old lady, taking her a drawing or cookies; (d) helping to carry some of the boy's belongings. Students may then write an appropriate response and color each picture.

Page 129 – Support Reconciliation
- Read the definition and discuss it with the students.
- Read the scenario and discuss it.
- Allow the students to complete the worksheet as directed, concentrating particularly on Question 4. Selected students may perform their "puppet reconciliation play" for the class.

Page 130 – Contribute to Research
- Discuss charities which students may be familiar with and any fund-raising days or activities which they may have participated in.
- Brainstorm and list any diseases or causes which students may feel are important to raise money for. Students may choose to create a research fund for diseases or causes from this list.
- Students complete the worksheet as directed.

Page 131 – Support Freedom
- The story is intended to make students aware of the difference between being free and captive. In the case of Kila, the lion cub, the students may realize that for some animals being caged may mean the difference between survival and extinction.
- Read and discuss the story and allow students to answer the Question 2.
- Discuss how students would feel to be an animal living in a cage in a zoo. Talk about people living in other countries who are not allowed the freedoms which are available to students living in a "free" country. The students may then complete Question 4.

Page 132 – Strive for Peace
- What is peace?
- What does peace mean to you?
- Read the information and look at the symbols.
- Discuss different things which may be used to symbolize peace. Some suggestions may be a clear, blue sky; quiet lake; a rainbow; or a sleeping child. List some ideas on the board for students to consider.
- Allow students to complete the worksheet as directed and share their designs when finished.

Graphic Organizer Example

Evaluation Charts

Plus	Minus	Interesting

PMI Chart

Positive (+)	Negative (−)
Plus	Negative
or	or
Like	Dislike
or	or
Agree	Disagree

Plus/Minus T-Chart

Can't Help Myself - Bad Habits!

Often little things that we do can annoy or irritate other people. We should try to change these bad habits so that we are behaving responsibly (sensibly).

1. Complete the table.

Bad Habit	How Does This Affect Other People?	How Could This Bad Habit Be Changed?
always pushing to be at the front of the line		
leaving pens and equipment all over the table		
kicking the table or tapping foot while others are working		

2. Discuss some other bad habits with a partner.

3. Complete the sentences.

　(a) Sometimes I annoy people when I ... _____

　　_____

　(b) I could change this by ... _____

　　_____

　(c) I get annoyed when people ... _____

　　_____

　(d) They could change this by ... _____

　　_____

Authority Figures

authority: *noun* the right to determine, judge or settle; the right to control or command; an accepted source of information or advice; an expert on a subject.

1. Draw and label people you know who are examples of each of these types of people.

a person who judges	a person who commands
a person who gives advice	an expert on something

respect: *noun* high regard; esteem; honor; respectful or friendly words of praise.

2. Choose one of the people above and write one way to show respect for him/her.

_____

_____

_____

_____

The Rules of the Game

1. Look at the board game.

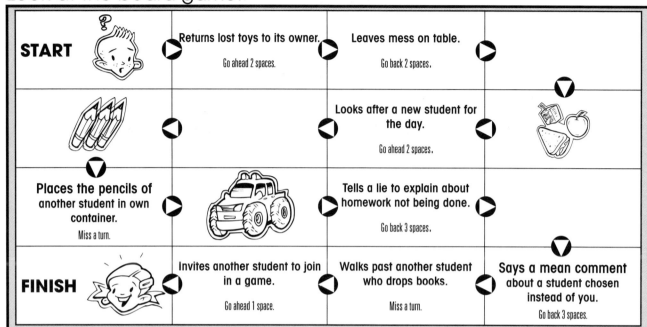

2. Write four or five simple rules for playing the game. Think about how many players there are, how to get the first player started, why a player has to miss a turn or moves backward or forward, and how you will know who is the winner.

(a) _____

_____

(b) _____

_____

(c) _____

_____

(d) _____

_____

(e) _____

_____

The Shepherd Boy

1. Read the fable.

> **T**here was once a shepherd boy whose job was to look after the sheep who grazed at the bottom of a mountain, near a forest.
>
> The shepherd boy often felt very lonely staying by himself all day, so he thought of a plan to get some of the villagers to keep him company and also bring some excitement to the dull village life.
>
> He rushed into the village shouting "Wolf! Wolf!" The villagers came out to see what was going on and some even stayed for a while to comfort him. The boy was so pleased with the way his plan had worked that he did it again a few days later. Again the villagers all came out to help. They began to realize that he was playing a trick on them.
>
> Soon after, a wolf came out of the forest and began to stalk the sheep. The boy yelled "Wolf! Wolf!" very loudly. The villagers thought that he was playing a trick on them again, so they ignored him. The wolf attacked and ate some sheep because no one came to stop him. The boy complained very loudly to all the villagers, but one wise man said to him:
>
> **"A person who lies won't be believed even when he tells the truth!"**

2. Answer the questions.

   (a) Why did the shepherd boy lie to the villagers?

   _____

   _____

   (b) Is it ever okay to lie? Circle **Yes** or **No**. Discuss this with a partner.

   (c) Write one reason why it is better to be honest than to lie.

   _____

   _____

What's the Right Thing to Do?

Read and discuss the scenarios to decide what is the right thing to do.

1. You are walking to school and see some money fall out of the bag of the girl in front of you.

   What is the right thing to do?

2. Your sister has lots of homework to do and asks you to do her chores at home.

   What is the right thing to do?

3. Dad is really tired after work and the dog is annoying him to be taken for a walk.

   What is the right thing to do?

4. One of your classmates is struggling to carry all of his things into the classroom.

   What is the right thing to do?

5. One of the children from another class is watching while you play in the sandbox. There are no buckets or shovels left.

   What is the right thing to do?

6. Children are hurrying to line up to use the climbing equipment. One smaller child behind you is pushed out of line by a bigger child.

   What is the right thing to do?

7. Two children are carrying the class lunches in the cafeteria basket. One child has his hands full of lunches which will not fit in the basket.

   What is the right thing to do?

8. One of the children at your table uses all of her paint but has not finished her picture. You still have a lot of paint left over.

   What is the right thing to do?

9. The teacher gives out books to a small group of children to follow while she reads. One child misses out on a book.

   What is the right thing to do?

10. During soccer practice, you accidentally knock over another child and he begins to cry.

    What is the right thing to do?

11. Mom has come home from work late. She still has to bring in the mail and the dry clothes, the kitchen trashcan needs to be emptied and some groceries need to be put away.

    What is the right thing to do?

12. Your little brother is grumbling about going to bed. Your parents are getting really annoyed with him. He likes to listen to you read.

    What is the right thing to do?

Be Useful

1. Write information to complete each column to show how you are useful or could be useful in each place.

Home	School	Community

2. Write reasons to explain WHY it is good to do things to be useful in each place.

Home	School	Community

3. Compare your answers with a partner or in a group, then write some other suggestions on how to be more useful in each place.

Home	School	Community

Community Event

It is important to be proud of your own community and to support the activities which take place there.

1. Complete the information for an advertisement for a local community event.

(a) What is the name of the event?	
(b) When is it being held?	
(c) Where is it being held?	
(d) What activities are going to happen there?	
(e) How much does it cost?	
(f) Who should people contact to find out more about the event?	
(g) What colorful illustrations or headings would make your advertisement more interesting?	

2. Create your advertisement on a separate sheet of paper.

Be a Fair Person

1. Read the information.

A fair person:

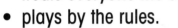

- treats other people the way they would like to be treated.
- thinks about how their actions will affect other people.
- doesn't blame other people for their own mistakes.
- listens to other people with an open mind.
- doesn't take advantage of other people.
- treats everyone the same.
- plays by the rules.
- takes turns.

2. Discuss the information in small groups and cross out any you don't agree with.

3. Write the ones which you think you need to improve on the "fair person" shape.

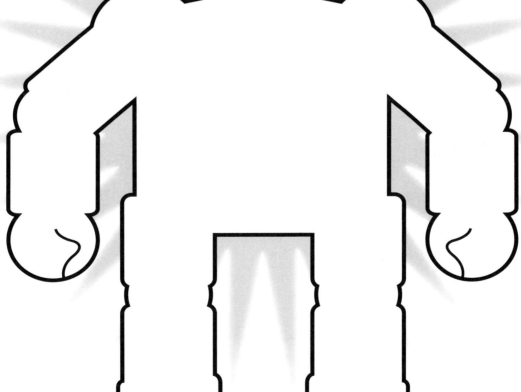

Care for Those Who Need Help

Look at the pictures and write one way to care for the people who need help.

A

B

C

D

128

Reconciliation

reconcile: *verb* to bring harmony or agreement between two groups who have been arguing for a long time.

1. Read the scenario.

> aria and Demetri are in the same class at school. They also live next door to each other. They used to walk together to school.
>
> One day, Demetri was playing with some other boys in the playground when they began to tease some of the girls, including Maria. Most of the girls took no notice of the teasing, but Maria was upset. When Demetri came to walk to school with her the next day, she told him that her mom was walking with her and she did not want him to come with them.
>
> She did not walk to school with him or talk to him for a very long time.

2. Color the pictures of Maria and Demetri and glue them to card stock.

3. When they are dry, cut them out and glue them to a craft stick.

4. Use them as puppets to work out a reconciliation (agreement) which helps them to be friends again.

My Research Fund

Answer the questions about an imaginary research fund or cause.

1. What disease, sickness, or cause would your fund like to support?	
2. What is the name of your fund?	
3. Where will you get the money to use for research?	
4. What activities will you put on to raise money for your research fund?	
5. Do you have a logo for your fund? If so, draw it or create one.	
6. Do you have a mascot for your research fund? If so, write its name and draw a picture of it.	
7. Do you have a celebrity who helps to raise money for your fund? If so, write their name.	

Kila's Story

1. Read the story.

K ila, the new lion cub, watched the groups of people as they came to stand near the fence of his enclosure. The adults pointed and talked about him and his family. The children smiled or asked questions. Some even called out "Here kitty, kitty, kitty!" to him.

When too many people crowded the fence, Kila snuggled up close to his mom's side. Sometimes he scurried into the long grasses to hide and peered at them through the stalks. He even tried growling at them like his mom, but it sounded more like a "meow" than a roar.

The keepers gave them plenty of food and clean water to drink. Kila's mom and dad were content with their home because it looked just like their "real" home. They had a lot of room to prowl and rocks to sleep near in the sun. The vet came regularly to see if they were well. Kila got lots of attention because he was the youngest.

One day, as the crowds pushed in, he saw a little boy with blonde streaky hair staring at him through the bars. Kila was used to people staring, but this little boy looked so sad as he watched him.

2. Answer the questions.

(a) What was good about Kila and his family living in the zoo?

_____

_____

_____

(b) Why do you think the little boy looked sad?

_____

_____

_____

3. Discuss with a partner how you would feel if you were an animal who had to live in a zoo. Think about some of the reasons why animals are placed in zoos.

Peace Symbol Mobile

Many years ago, people who were worried about wars displayed peace signs and symbols during marches and on posters. Some peace symbols are shown below. Design your own peace symbol mobile using the steps below.

1. What symbol will you use for peace?

   _____

2. Why did you choose this symbol?

   _____

   _____

   _____

3. How many symbols will you need to make your mobile? What size (or sizes) will they need to be?

   _____

   _____

4. How will you hang your mobile?

   _____

   _____

   _____

5. What materials will you need to make your mobile?

   _____

   _____

   _____

   _____

6. Draw and label a picture of your finished design.

AND I LOVE LIFE!

THE SIX KINDS OF BEST

KIND TO OTHERS
KIND TO YOURSELF
KIND TO THE ENVIRONMENT
BE
KIND THE LEARNING
KIND THE ACHIEVING
KIND THE COMMUNITY

VALUES EDUCATION PROGRAM

And I ...	Point to yourself and touch your chest.	
love ...	Hug yourself.	
life!	Hands and arms outstretched above your head.	

A chatterbox is a fun method to reinforce concepts as well as to engage learners who utilize the visual/spatial, verbal/linguistic, logical/mathematical and bodily/kinesthetic intelligences, while encouraging the interpersonal intelligence.

Use the pattern given to encourage students to make individual chatterboxes relating to specific areas of this book. A specific example is given on page 135.

Instructions

❶ Begin with a square piece of paper or light card stock.

❷ Fold in the corners so that they meet in the center of the square.

❸ Turn over and repeat the procedure, folding corners in to meet at the center. This will create four triangular flaps.

❹ Number each half of the triangular "flaps" (eight in all). Any numbers can be used. Also number each of the four square flaps on the underside of the construction.

❺ Fold the chatterbox in half, so that the numbered squares are on the outside.

❻ Place thumbs and forefingers under the square flaps. Move thumbs and forefingers in an "open/shut" motion. This will mean the chatterbox opens and shuts, revealing the eight "triangular" numbers each time.

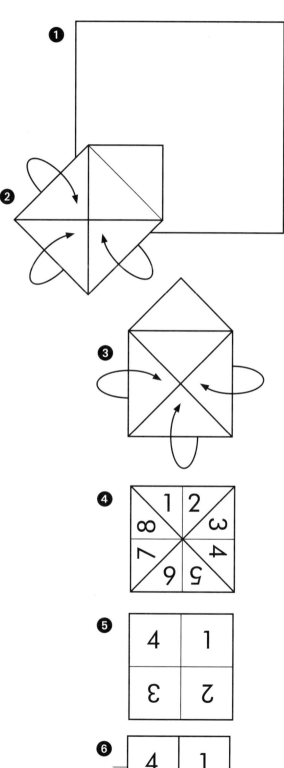

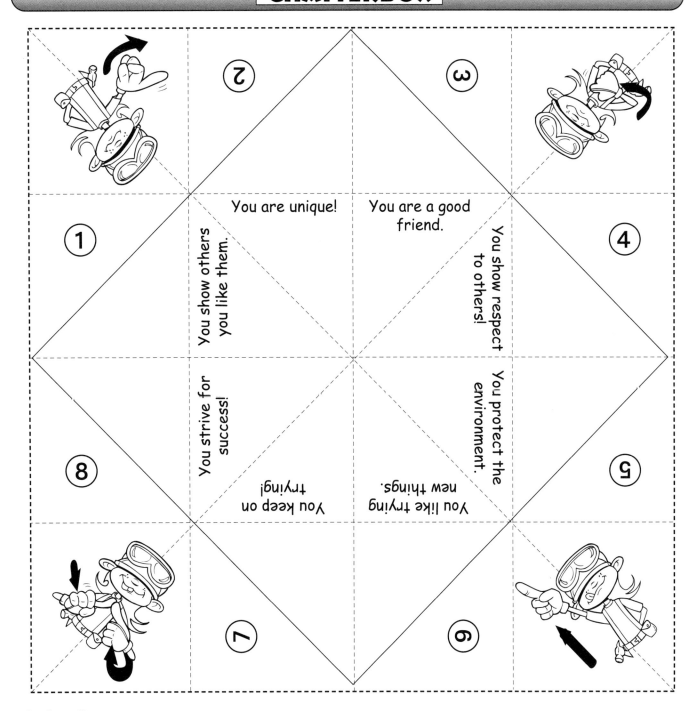

Instructions

1. Cut out the square.
2. Place the square with the written side down and fold as directed on page 134.
3. To use with a partner:
   - Ask your partner to select an affirmation and "open and close" according to the number of words or syllables.
   - Ask your partner to select a number and "open and close" the chatterbox the given number of times.
   - Ask your partner to choose a number and open to reveal a nice comment about themselves!

Books

The 7 Habits of Highly Effective People *by Stephen Covey*

Six Thinking Hats *by Edward De Bono*

Taxonomy of Educational Objectives *by Benjamin Bloom*

Revised Bloom's Taxonomy *by Lorin Anderson*

The Tipping Point *by Malcolm Gladwell*

Multiple Intelligences *Published by World Teachers Press®*

Conflict Resolution *Published by World Teachers Press®*

Me *Published by World Teachers Press®*

Healthy Choices *Published by World Teachers Press®*

Web Sites

www.charactercounts.org/

www.cyh.com/HealthTopicsAlpha.aspx2p=237

www.goodcharacter.com

www.kidshealth.com/kid/feeling/

(Note: Web sites correct at time of publication.)

(*Six Kinds of Best Values Education Program* http://www.sixkindsofbest.com)